God's Covenant with Animals
A Biblical Basis for the Humane
Treatment of All Creatures

Whenever the rainbow appears in the clouds I will see it and
remember the everlasting covenant between God and all
living creatures of every kind on the earth.

Genesis 9:16

J. R. Hyland

Lantern Books—New York
A Division of Booklight Inc.

2000
Lantern Books
One Union Square West, Suite 201
New York, NY 10003

Copyright © J. R. Hyland 2000, 2004

Reprinted, 2001, 2004

Printed in the United States of America

printed on 100% post-consumer waste paper, chlorine-free

This book is dedicated to the Reverend James Thompson, an Anglican priest known as "the Animals' Padre." In both his ministry to the animals and his ministry to people, he has always chosen to follow the Gospel of Christ rather than the doctrines of men.

Contents

By the Same Author

Sexism Is a Sin: The Biblical Basis of Female Equality

Acknowledgment

Acknowledgment is made to the following for permission to use copyrighted materials.

Viatoris Publications for text from "The Slaughter of Terrified Beasts," copyright 1988, Sarasota, FL.

Humane Religion for excerpted material from Vol 2, #3, copyrighted under the title "Jews, Christians and Hunting." www.humanereligion.com

I would like to acknowledge the pioneering work of Hans Ruesch, author of *Slaughter of the Innocent* and *Naked Empress*. His integrity and refusal to yield to self-serving speciesism in the struggle against vivisection is unsurpassed—and, for the most part, unmatched.

Terminology

Although contemporary religious studies avoid using gender specific terms when referring to God, no such effort is made in traditional Christian churches. Neither do such churches accept the current use of C.E. (Common Era) or B.C.E. (Before the Common Era) as replacements for A.D. or B.C. Because this book deals with conventional Christian beliefs, traditional usage is retained, as is the use of "Man," as a general term, when appropriate. Through the centuries both Judaism and Christianity have excluded women from their rituals and from the formulation of doctrine. Thus, to use the word *humankind* can be just as misleading as it is to subsume women under the term *mankind*.

Abbreviations used with Scripture quotations:
AMP—The Amplified Bible
JB—The Jerusalem Bible
NAS—The New American Standard
NEB—The New English Bible
NIV—The New International Version
When no abbreviation is used, the King James version of the Bible is being quoted.

Quotations

When man diverted from the path [of goodness] the animals followed him.... If man now would rise to his original nature and would not do evil any longer, then the animals too would return to their original gentle nature.

Theophilus, Bishop of Antioch (A.D. 150)

Oh God, enlarge within us the sense of fellowship with all living things, our brothers the animals to whom Thou gavest the earth as their home in common with us. We remember with shame that in the past we have exercised the high dominion of man with ruthless cruelty so that the voice of the earth, which should have gone up to Thee in song, has been a groan of travail.

St. Basil, Archbishop of Caesarea (A.D. 275)

Surely we ought to show kindness and gentleness to animals for many reasons, and chiefly because they are of the same Source as ourselves.

St. John Chrysostom (A.D. 400)

All the creatures—not the higher creatures alone, but also the lower, according to that which each of them has received in itself from God—each one raises its voice in testimony to that which God is...each one after its manner exalts God, since it has God in itself.

St. John of the Cross (1582)

Not to hurt our humble brethren [the animals] is our first duty to them, but to stop there is not enough. We have a higher mission: to be of service to them whenever they require it.

St. Francis of Assisi

When a man becomes accustomed to have pity upon animals...his soul will likewise grow accustomed to be kind to human beings.

Sefer Ha Chinuch, Mitzvah 596

All goodness is a participation in God and His love for His creatures. God loves irrational creatures and His love provides for them.

St. Catherine of Genoa

I believe in my heart that faith in Jesus Christ can and will lead us beyond an exclusive concern for the well-being of other human beings to a broader concern for the well-being of the birds in our backyards, the fish in our rivers, and every living creature on the face of the earth.

John Wesley

Love the world with an all-embracing love. Love the animals; God has given them the rudiments of thought and joy untroubled. Do not trouble them, do not harass them, do not deprive them of their happiness, do not work against God's intent. Man, do not pride yourself on your superiority to them, for they are without sin, and you with your greatness defile the earth.

Fyodor Dostoyevsky

Cruelty to animals is as if man did not love God . . . there is something so dreadful, so Satanic, in tormenting those who have never harmed us, and who cannot defend themselves, who are utterly in our power.

Cardinal John Henry Newman

We are compelled by the commandment of love contained in our hearts and thought, and proclaimed by Jesus, to give rein to our natural sympathy for animals. We are also compelled to help them and spare them suffering.

Albert Schweitzer

Animals, as part of God's creation, have rights which must be respected. It behoves us always to be sensitive to their needs and to the reality of their pain.

Dr. Donald Coggan, Archbishop of Canterbury

The true God is love, goodness, and mercy—not sacrifice, cruelty, killing, and murder. . . . We shall not kill or sacrifice other creatures for him; we shall only sacrifice ourselves for our human and animal brothers.

Reverend Carl A. Skriver

Early in my life I came to the conclusion that there was no basic difference between man and animals. If a man has the heart to cut the throat of a chicken or a calf, there's no reason he should not be willing to cut the throat of a man.

Isaac Bashevis Singer

It is time, fully time, that all Christian people awake to the necessity of taking an active part in the fight against what I dare to call the Crime of Animal Cruelty. Everyone who loves God and animals should help bear the burden of the fight against this insidious evil.

Right Reverend John Chandler White

In the end, a lack of regard for the life and well-being of an animal must bring with it a lowering of man's self-respect, and it is integral to our Christian faith that this world is God's world and that man is a trustee and steward of God's creation who must render up an account for his stewardship.

Dr. Robert Runcie, Archbishop of Canterbury

[St. Francis] looked upon creation with the eyes of one who could recognize in it the marvelous work of the hand of God. His solicitous care, not only towards men, but also towards animals is a faithful echo of the love with which God in the beginning pronounced his "fiat" which brought them into existence. We too are called to a similar attitude.

Pope John Paul II

Quotations

To stand for Christ is to stand against the evil of cruelty inflicted on those who are weak, vulnerable, unprotected, undefended, morally innocent, and in that class we must unambiguously include animals.

The Reverend Andrew Linzey

We cannot treat any living thing callously, and we are responsible for what happens to other beings, human or animal, even if we do not personally come into contact with them.

Rabbi Pinchas Peli

Animals are part of God's creation and people have special responsibilities to them. The Jewish tradition clearly indicates that we are forbidden to be cruel to animals and that we are to treat them with compassion.

Richard H. Schwartz

Part One: Prologue

P ROGRESSIVE REVELATION IS A CONCEPT ACCEPTED by theologians of diverse backgrounds and loyalties. It has to do with the belief that although God's self-revelation does not change, the human capacity to receive that revelation does change. It grows and develops as people progress in their ability to understand who God is and what constitutes right relationship to the Creator.

This progressive understanding led to the repudiation of human sacrifices as well as to the progress from polytheistic to monotheistic belief. And in the time of the Latter Prophets of Israel, the concept of social justice as a measure of righteousness and conformity with the will of God came to the fore. Prophets like Isaiah, Jeremiah, Micah, and Amos told their people that the true worship of God manifested itself in the just and compassionate treatment of the helpless and powerless, not in ceremonial or sacrificial rituals. The revelation given by those prophets also concerned mankind's relationship to animal life.

1

The abuse of animals—like the oppression of human beings—is opposed to the way of life that God has ordained. And although the world has fallen far short of the standards given by God, the Prophetic Age signaled that it was time for the human race to remember its beginnings. It was time to try to live the kind of life that God ordained at the Creation.

Through the prophets, God called the people to "beat their swords into plowshares" (Isa. 2:4) and promised a better world if they did not "oppress the alien, the orphan, or the widow." (Jer. 7:6) A world of justice and nonviolence was also a world that did not abuse animals in the name of their Creator. There was to be no more sacrifice of animals on the altars of God: "I have no pleasure in the blood of lambs and goats. . . . Take your evil deeds out of my sight." (Isa. 1:11,16)

The advent of the Prophetic Age in Israel marked a milestone in the spiritual journey of the people of God. There was a breakthrough in consciousness and a call to justice, mercy, and compassion that still sounds in our own day. But today—as in biblical times—there is still an adamant refusal to follow that call. There is still a reactionary effort to make the worship of God a thing of ceremony and ritual rather than a matter of compassionate treatment for all creatures.

But there are those who struggle to build a world of peace, justice, and compassion for all forms of life. They try to walk in the light that the Spirit shines into our darkness. That Spirit continually seeks to lead the human race out of the violence and selfishness that made a hell out of the paradise that God prepared for all creatures.

Chapter One
Animal Sacrifice

THE EIGHTH CENTURY B.C. INAUGURATED AN ERA of spiritual and moral evolution in Judaism that struggles to continue in our own day. It was a giant leap in consciousness that seemed to emerge, full-blown, in the teachings of the Latter Prophets.

The teachings of those men affirmed the primary importance of social justice, rejected ceremonial and sacrificial religion, and articulated a change from henotheism to monotheism. They also taught that *homo sapiens* is not the end-all or be-all of God's creation—that, in fact, the animal kingdom is an integral part of the Kingdom to come. It would be a peaceable kingdom where "they shall not hurt or destroy in all my holy mountain: for the earth shall be full of the knowledge of the Lord." (Isa. 11:9)

Although this change in consciousness regarding animals was first articulated in the Hebrew Scriptures (or Old

Testament), students of religion have traditionally credited India with the concept. They point to the teachings of Buddha and Mahavira, both of whom denounced the sacrifice of animals in the sixth century B.C. The Hinduism of their day required the slaughter of sacrificial animals; it was an integral part of that religion.

As is usual in a sacrificial cult, the priests wielded great power. The power of the Brahmin priests rested on the teaching that only they could offer the kind of sacrifices that were "the atonement for everything . . . the sacrifice that redeems all sin."[1] Only the priests were empowered to utter the sacred formula over such sacrifices; they were the intermediaries between the gods and men. They alone could ensure that the gods were propitiated and that petitions would be granted. Without their mediation the people would be lost—they would be out of favor with the forces on whom they thought their very lives depended.

Of course, the priests were not going to accept any teaching that repudiated the animal sacrifice that was the cornerstone of their power. Consequently, they saw Buddha and Mahavira as enemies. Not only did these sages teach that sacrificial worship did not secure the blessings of any god, they also taught that such sacrifices were intrinsically evil. They taught that inflicting pain and death on other sentient creatures retarded the spiritual growth of human beings. Since animals are equipped with the same five senses as human beings, they could obviously experience the same sensations of pain, suffering, and fear. To abuse these creatures in the name of any god was an affront to the concept of Deity.

Because these teachings against sacrifice could not be contained within the Hinduism of their time, they became part of the separate religions of Buddhism and Jainism. When that happened, the substance of these new teachings stood out in clear distinction from Hindu doctrine. As these new religions developed, the concept of nonviolence toward man and all other creatures was reinforced.

But India was not the setting for the first religious reaction against animal sacrifice. The understanding that the suffering and death of animals was repugnant to the Creator had surfaced among the Hebrews long before Indian sages articulated such concepts. Beginning with Isaiah in 750 B.C., the Latter Prophets condemned animal sacrifice. In so doing these prophets were reiterating the ancient knowledge found in Genesis: Animals were created in love and goodness, just as human beings had been. And humans were ordained to be the loving caretakers of animals, not their cruel abusers.

Although the Judaic prophecies regarding animals and their treatment predated the teachings in India, the message of the Latter Prophets did not stand out in clear relief because their teachings did not break from Judaism to form a separate belief system. Instead, their prophetic message was absorbed into the mainstream of the Hebrew religion and became still another current running through the spiritual history of Israel. Consequently, the warnings against sacrificial religion continued to coexist with a priestly power structure that was still developing complex rituals for slaughter.

This coexistence of opposing viewpoints is a great strength of the Old Testament; it is one of the reasons for its continuing impact on the human race. The Hebrew Scriptures record both the continuity and the changes that took place in Judaism's understanding of God. They tell of the struggle between opposing values that continued for many centuries. The

Scriptures also provide a continuous, if selective, chronicle of a nation's spiritual journey.

The Old Testament does not gloss over the negative history of its people. The good and the bad, the going forward and the sliding back, the high points of the nation's history and its nadir—all are included in the record. But in reading this record it is important to understand that negative developments do not always receive a negative comment. Often, it is only when a later generation adds to the biblical record that it becomes evident that certain events had not received the unqualified endorsement that earlier accounts seemed to present. The story of Jacob and Esau is a case in point.

Although Jacob cheated his brother of his birthright, the original account in the book of Genesis does not comment negatively on the fact that he deliberately cheated his brother. But hundreds of years after the fact, the Bible does refer to Jacob's deception as something blameworthy. (See Isa. 43:27; Jer. 9:4; Hos. 12:2–3 AMP.)

This negative assessment of Jacob's action was not a new thought in Judaism; it had long been present in Israel's discussions and disputations of the incident. Eventually this negative judgment of the event became part of the biblical record.

The same kind of deferred judgment occurs regarding the sacrifice of animals. For centuries the Scriptures presented a seemingly one-sided view of the practice—a view that implied sacrifice was unquestioningly accepted in Israel. But during that time there was an undercurrent that opposed such worship. And with the advent of the Prophet Isaiah in the eighth century B.C., that current surfaced and entered the mainstream of

Hebrew life. Opposition to the entrenched rituals of sacrificial worship then became part of the biblical record.

Because widely divergent viewpoints like these can only appear as contradictions in a short-term view of events, an overview of the Bible is necessary. An overview provides a long-term perspective. We see that it is conflict—not contradiction—that the Bible is reporting. Many ideals struggled for supremacy in Judaism over the centuries, and the various books of the Old Testament provide different perspectives on those conflicts.

Without an overview and without a knowledge of the deferred judgment that is applied to some biblical events, it would seem that suddenly, for no discernible reason, there was a reaction in Judaism against the sacrifice of animals. This sudden reaction would be doubly confusing because at the time that the prophets began speaking out against the slaughter, the cult of Temple worship was at a zenith. And the ritual slaughter of animals was at the heart of that worship.

The priests who officiated at the sacrifices had enormous religious and political power. Like their Hindu counterparts, the Israelite priests had a vested interest in sacrificial worship. They had developed complex and intricate rituals for slaughter, all with appropriate prayers to God. Those rituals had become completely integrated into their sacred tradition.

By the time Isaiah began his prophetic ministry, slaughtering animals in the name of God had assumed the nature of an additional commandment in the eyes of the people. But Isaiah, and those who followed him, called the people back from their violent worship. The Lord, they said, had never asked for the slaughter of His own creatures: It was Man himself who had instituted sacrificial worship.

The prophets also tried to reestablish the teaching contained in the book of beginnings—the book of Genesis. Genesis taught that animals, like human beings, were created by God; that God had concern for their welfare, just as He had for human welfare. And as surely as the Lord had established a covenant with human creatures, so He had also covenanted with other creatures—with the beasts of the field and the birds of the air.[2]

The prophecies of men like Isaiah, Micah, and Amos reiterated that the sacrifice of animals was an abomination in the sight of God, an unholy practice that demanded repentance. Isaiah was the first of his era to prophesy against the sacrificial cult:

> The multitude of your sacrifices—what are they to me? says the Lord. I have more than enough of burnt offerings of rams and the fat of fattened animals; I have no pleasure in the blood of bulls and lambs and goats. . . . Your hands are full of blood; wash and make yourselves clean. Take your evil deeds out of my sight. (Isa. 1:11, 15–16 NIV)

Jeremiah, Amos, and Hosea were equally vocal about the evils of animal sacrifice. They all spoke out in the name of God against the killing taking place on the altars:

> For Ephraim in his sin has multiplied altars, altars have become his sin. Though they sacrifice flesh as offerings to me and eat them, I the Lord will not accept them. Their guilt will be remembered and their sins punished. They shall go back to Egypt. . . . (Hos. 8:11–13 NEB)

They would "go back to Egypt" because, when they lived in captivity there, the sacrificial cult was not yet an established

Hebrew tradition. The prophet knew his people had to go back in their understanding to a time when they had not been conditioned to accept animal sacrifice as a necessary part of their worship.

The prophet Jeremiah also addressed this issue of the development of sacrificial worship and pointed back to the time when the Hebrews were first freed from their captivity in Egypt:

> Thus says the Lord of hosts, the God of Israel: Add your burnt offerings to your sacrifices and eat flesh. For I did not speak to your fathers, or command them in the day that I brought them out of the land of Egypt, concerning burnt offerings and sacrifices. But this is what I commanded them saying, "Obey My voice and I will be your God and you will walk in all the way which I command you, that it may be well with you." Yet they did not obey or incline their ear, but walked in their own counsels and in the stubbornness of their own heart, and went backward and not forward. Since the day that your fathers came out of the land of Egypt until this day. . . . (Jer. 7:21–25 NAS)

The Prophet Amos raised his voice in condemnation of sacrificial worship. He, too, reminded the people of the time when their ancestors left Egypt; a time when the rituals of animal sacrifice had not yet become a cornerstone of their sacred tradition. During the forty years of wandering in the wilderness they were taken care of by God—there was no need for elaborate ceremonies and festivals. Speaking in the name of the Lord, Amos forcefully declared:

> I hate and despise your feasts, I take no pleasure in your solemn festivals. When you offer me holocausts, I reject your oblations, and refuse to look at your sacrifices of fattened

cattle . . . but let justice flow like water, and integrity like an unfailing stream. Did you bring me sacrifice and oblation in the wilderness for all those forty years, House of Israel? (Amos 5:21–22, 24–25 JB)

If the chosen people were to continue their spiritual leadership, they would have to accept the prophets' message. They would have to accept that God was not pleased by a worship in which His creatures were dragged, in a frenzy, to be slaughtered in His name.

The Prophet Jeremiah voiced God's indictment of the human race as a species that took advantage of the most helpless in its midst—a race that abused those without the power to protect themselves. He juxtaposed the abuse of powerless humans with the slaughter of helpless animals on the altars of the Temple:

Thus says the Lord of Hosts, the God of Israel: Amend your ways. . . . Do not trust in deceptive words saying, This is the temple of the Lord, the temple of the Lord, the temple of the Lord! . . . [but] if you do not oppress the alien, the orphan or the widow and do not shed innocent blood in this place . . . then I will let you dwell in the land that I gave to your fathers. . . . (Jer. 7:3–4, 6–7 NAS)

The call for the rejection of animal sacrifice was also the call for a religion marked by social justice. Ceremonies, sacrifices, and religious feast days were not pleasing to the Lord. The relief of the sufferings of the helpless and the oppressed constituted the true worship of God:

What are your multiplied sacrifices to me? . . . I take no pleasure in the blood of bulls, lambs or goats. . . . I hate your new moon and your appointed feasts. . . . Cease to do evil. Learn to do good; seek justice; reprove the ruthless. Defend the orphan; plead for the widows. . . . (Isa. 1:11, 14, 16–17 NAS)

Not only did the prophets point out that sacrifices and ceremonies were man-made substitutes for the true worship of God, they also faced their people with the fact that the violence done to sacrificial animals was reflected in the violence that human beings were willing to inflict on each other. And slaughtering animals, as an act of worship among the Hebrews, was eventually reflected in the practice of human sacrifice.

Although Judaism never condoned human sacrifice, by the time of the Latter Prophets the sacrifice even of their own children had become widespread among the people. Some of those who believed that God was pleased by the slaughter of animals eventually concluded that He would be even more pleased by the sacrifice of human flesh—the flesh of their own children.

In the Book of Micah, that prophet made the connection between the sacrifice of human flesh and the sacrifice of animals:

With what shall I come before the Lord. . . . Shall I come to Him with burnt offerings, with yearling calves? Does the Lord take delight in thousands of rams, in ten thousand rivers of oil: *Shall I present my firstborn for my rebellious acts, the fruit of my body for the sin of my soul?* He has told you, O man what is good . . . do justice, to love kindness, and to walk humbly with your God. (Mic. 6:6–8 NIV emphasis added)

In their oracles, the Latter Prophets frequently connected man's violence toward animals with the violence he directed toward other people. Just as frequently, they linked a world of peace and prosperity with a world where animals, as well as human beings, would be free from exploitation.

A peaceable world was necessarily a world in which no creature would destroy or be destroyed. It was a world where all could live their lives in security and safety. The eleventh chapter of Isaiah describes this peaceable kingdom as a time and place wherein the human race will strive to live in accord with the Divinity in whose image it was created. And in that kind of world, the animal kingdom will reflect the goodness and mercy that will be the hallmark of human affairs:

> . . . with righteousness He will judge the needy, with justice. He will give decisions for the poor of the earth. . . . The wolf will live with the lamb, the leopard will lie down with the goat and the calf and the lion and the yearling together: and a little child will lead them. (Isa. 11:4, 6 NIV)

The prophet went on to further describe this peace that will be evident among the animals as well as among men:

> The cow and the bear make friends, their young lie down together. The lion eats straw like the ox. The infant plays over the cobra's hole; into the viper's lair the young child puts his hand. They do not hurt, nor harm, on all my holy mountain, for the country is filled with the knowledge of the Lord as the waters swell the sea. (Isa. 11:7–9 JB)

This knowledge that fills the world "as the waters swell the sea" is the knowledge of a rule of justice and compassion. It is a rule that people will finally accept; a rule that rejects the unjust and violent behavior that human beings demonstrated so often.

Like Isaiah, the Prophet Micah spoke of a time when people will be willing to put into practice what they learn—a time when they will act in a way that conforms to the way God would have things done:

> Come and let us go to the mountain of the Lord and to the house of the God of Jacob, that He may teach us about His ways. . . . Then they will hammer their swords into plowshares and their spears into pruning hooks; nation will not lift up sword against nation. And never again will they train for war. And each of them will sit under his vine and under his fruit tree with no one to make them afraid. (Mic. 4:2–4, NAS)

Still another of the prophets—Hosea—prophesied that there would be no more war. There would be no war because human behavior would be marked by love and compassion. It would be a time when men and women would renounce their violence because they had had enough of the misery and suffering they had created. And in a world marked by love and compassion, human beings would not only live in peace with each other, they would also live in peace with the beasts of the fields and the birds of the air:

> In that day I will make a covenant for them with the beasts of the field and the birds of the air and the creatures that move along the ground. Bow and sword and battle I will abolish from the land so that all may lie down in safety. I will betroth you to me forever; I will betroth you in righteousness and justice, in love and compassion. (Hos. 2:18–19 NIV)

13

The prophets taught that God's blessings would abound only in a world where human beings rejected violence and "no longer taught war." But the journey toward that peaceable kingdom demanded that the sacrifice of animals stop. A people who remained insensitive to the travesty of a worship that called for the terrorizing and slaughter of other creatures was a people whose spiritual development was being retarded; a people who had not yet taken their first step toward a millennial world.

Amazingly, though the Latter Prophets called for the reform or abolition of many of the institutions and practices that had been sanctified by the Hebrews, their message survived in the scriptures of their people. Their words were preserved because they spoke to Judaism's deepest roots. These men of God had not introduced new concepts into Israel; they had reintroduced themes that went back to the very beginning—back to the time of Genesis. And their great age of prophecy was a sign that it was time for the human race to recover its spiritual heritage. Speaking in the name of God, the prophets let the people know that it was time for the world to once again reflect the qualities that God had ordained at the Creation—love, compassion, and mercy for all creatures.

---

1. John D. Noss. *Man's Religions*, 6th Ed. (New York: Macmillan Publishing Co., Inc., 1980), p. 83.
2. See Chapter Three, "After The Flood."

Chapter Two
In the Beginning

THE VISION OF THE LATTER PROPHETS—OF A TIME
when the lion will lie down with the lamb and all
earth's creatures will live in peace with each other—
seems an impossible dream. It seems impossible because
human beings have chosen to believe that both animals and
people are violent by nature. Since this is held to be a self-
evident truth, any information that casts doubt on its credibility
is rejected. So the creed remains intact; having evolved from
animals, the worst behavior of human beings simply confirms
the fact that they have not yet outgrown their barbarism.

This view of a world in the process of evolving from
barbarism to civilization can be a comforting one. No matter
how badly people or societies may behave, they have come a
long way from their primitive beginnings. Patience must be
exhibited with *homo sapiens*: Evolving from barbarism is no

easy task. The dogma is different for animals. It is generally believed that they were biologically doomed to violence, that their genes are somehow permanently programmed for killing. This belief system conveniently overlooks the facts of conditioning and adaptation. It dismisses the possibility that having become conditioned to violence, some species eventually adapted to such behavior.

The biblical view of natural history contradicts the theory that the human race has evolved over long periods of time to its present, higher, development. In fact, the Bible tells a story of regression, not progression.

The Book of Genesis reports that both animals and humans were created with a nonviolent nature, that goodness was their innate characteristic. Genesis tells the story of creatures whose natural condition is one of peaceful coexistence with their own species and with all other species. And although all have fallen from a higher state, their innate goodness—their nonviolent nature—remains waiting to be reactivated.

Even though they have adapted to a violent lifestyle, both animals and humans can readapt to their original peaceful natures. It is on this foundational truth that the millennial vision of the Latter Prophets was based. It was this truth that undergirded their vision of a time when, once again, humans and nonhumans would live together peaceably, in a peaceable world. It would be a world free from the fear and suffering that earth's creatures have unleashed upon themselves.

Like the prophets who linked the fate of men and animals in a millennial future, the Book of Genesis links them in their far-distant past. Both humans and animals were created as extensions of God's love and goodness. All creatures had within them the same "breath of life." (Gen.6:17) All were given the same instructions to "be fruitful and increase in number." In this picture of paradise, the man and woman were loving and trusted caregivers for the creatures among whom they lived. Theirs was a relationship of trust and leadership—not of dominance or exploitation.

The nonviolent nature of all earth's inhabitants is further delineated in the biblical report of God's plan for the sustenance of all creatures. Food was provided only from the bounty of the earth; no creature was to feed on another:

> Then God said [to the man and the woman], "I give you every seed-bearing plant on the face of the whole earth and every tree that has fruit with seed in it. They will be for your food. And to all the beasts of the earth and all the birds in the air and all the creatures that move on the ground—everything that has breath of life in it—I give every green plant for food." And it was so. God saw all that He had made and it was very good. (Gen. 1:29–31 NIV)

There is no information regarding the amount of time it took for this idyllic existence to end, but the third chapter of Genesis reports a degeneration that has already taken place. The man and woman have chosen to partake of evil; they have chosen to "know" good and evil (Gen. 3:22), where before they had "known" only the good.

Once they had chosen to know evil, the degeneration of Adam and Eve reached the point where they were no longer able to respect or abide by the rules of a paradisiacal existence. Consequently, they had to leave Eden. Their new environment reflected their regressive behavior.

Because humans were their leaders, the animals reflected their fall from a higher estate. In our age of ecological concern it is easier to understand how the negative behavior of human beings adversely affected the life around them. It reached the point that the very earth was "cursed":

> Cursed is the ground because of you . . . it will produce thorns and thistles for you and you will eat the plants of the fields by the sweat of your brow. (Gen. 3:17–19 NIV)

No longer would the lush bounty of earth automatically provide Adam and Eve with nourishment, and the animals would share the human fate of having to labor and forage for their food. Together all had enjoyed an Edenic existence; together they had deteriorated from their high estate. The Book of Genesis records that together they continued to deteriorate until, at last, the earth could no longer support the violence of its inhabitants. "The earth was corrupt in God's sight and full of violence." (Gen. 6:11)

> The Lord saw how great man's wickedness on the earth had become, and every inclination of the thoughts of his heart was only evil all the time. . . . So the Lord said: I will wipe mankind, whom I have created, from the face of the earth— man and animals and creatures that move along the ground and birds of the air—for I am grieved that I have made them. (Gen. 6:5, 7 NIV)

The waters of a great flood would wash away this uncivilized civilization. But a remnant would survive. The Lord spoke to Noah; he and his family would be saved from the coming catastrophe—however, there was a condition to be fulfilled: If they were to survive they had to fulfill their role as caregivers for the animals. Nonhumans as well as humans had to be provided with safe passage.

Noah's commission to provide for the animals is a story of crucial importance. The Bible has already told how God gave human beings responsibility for the care and welfare of other creatures at the time of Creation; how, by the time of the Flood, they had already corrupted themselves and abused that responsibility. Nevertheless, the Scriptures make it clear that accountability for the animals would continue to be a fact of human existence. Without safe passage for them, there would be no safe passage for Noah and his family.

It took a prodigious amount of time and work for Noah to construct something large enough to contain all the creatures who were to survive the Flood. It took an enormous effort for him to fulfill his responsibility as caregiver for the other creatures of earth. But if he and his family were to survive as a species, they had to fulfill their caregiving role. The animals who survived—like Noah and his family—were individually called to be saved from the Flood. God communicated His message to specific animals and, two by two, they presented themselves to Noah:

> And Noah and his sons and his wife and his sons' wives entered the ark to escape the waters of the flood. Pairs of clean and unclean animals, and of all creatures ... *came to Noah* and entered the ark. (Gen. 7:7, 8–9 NIV emphasis added)

> Pairs of all creatures that have the breath of life in them *came to Noah* and entered the Ark. (Gen. 7:15 NIV emphasis added)

Chapter Three
After the Flood

God remembered Noah and the wild animals and the
livestock that were with him in the ark and He sent a wind
over the earth and the waters receded. (Gen. 8:1 NIV)

G OD REMEMBERED NOAH AND THE WILD
animals." The biblical record of post-Flood events
begins with this continued revelation of God's equal
concern for human and nonhuman creatures. This theme is
repeated in the story of the descent from the ark.

Then God said to Noah, come out of the ark, you and your
wife and your sons and their wives. Bring out every kind of
living creature that is with you—the birds, the animals and
all the creatures that move along the ground—so they can
multiply on the earth and be fruitful and increase in number
on it. (Gen. 8:15–17 NIV)

God blessed Noah and his sons, saying to them, Be fruitful and fill the earth. (Gen. 9:1 NIV)

Both animals and men are commanded, "be fruitful and multiply." As in the creation account, birds, beasts, and human beings are given the same instructions. (Gen. 1:22, 28) This theme of equal treatment and equal concern is given an ultimate reinforcement in the story of the covenant that God made with earth's inhabitants after the Flood. In fact, the biblical passage that tells of this covenant is unique—it gives the same message five times in one paragraph. (Gen. 9:8–17)

In the Hebrew Scriptures, repetition is used to signal that what is being said is extremely important. In this case, the critical message repeated the fact that God was entering into a covenant relationship with animals as well as with men:

(1) This is the sign of the covenant I am making between Me and you and every living creature . . . a covenant for all generations to come. I have set My rainbow in the clouds and it will be the sign of the covenant. (Gen. 9:11–13 NIV)

(2) Then God said to Noah. . . . I now establish My covenant with you and your descendants after you and with every living creature that was with you—the birds, the livestock and all the wild animals, all those that came out of the ark with you—every living creature on earth. (Gen. 9:8–10 NIV)

(3) Whenever I bring clouds over the earth and the rainbow appears in the clouds I will see it and I will remember My covenant between Me and you and all living creatures of every kind. (Gen. 9:14–15 NIV)

(4) Whenever the rainbow appears in the clouds I will see it
and remember the everlasting covenant between God and all
living creatures of every kind on the earth. (Gen. 9:16 NIV)

(5) So God said to Noah, this is the sign of the covenant I
have established between Me and all life on earth. (Gen. 9:17
NIV)

The idea of covenanting with God is an exalted concept—a
sacred phenomenon. In biblical terms it constitutes a unique
relationship—a special bonding. And the constant repetition
that God made this special bond between Himself and the
animals came at a crucial point in the history of the earth. Just
as life after the Fall in Eden was life lived at a much regressed
level, so life after the Flood was a much lower order of existence
than it had been before.

The world that was washed away by the waters of the Flood
was a world that had nurtured and influenced all those who
survived in the ark; and it was a heritage of corruption and
degeneracy. The Amplified Bible most vividly presents the
extent of that decay, as it describes the world in which Noah
and the other survivors had lived.

The earth was depraved and putrid in God's sight and the
land was filled with violence (desecration, infringement,
outrage, assault, and lust for power). And God looked upon
the world and saw how degenerate, debased and vicious it
was, for all humanity had corrupted their way upon the earth
and lost their true direction. (Gen. 6:11–12)

This was the kind of world that had nurtured Noah and his
family. And this was the world in which Noah was outstanding

for his righteousness. The Bible tells why he was saved from the flood:

> Noah found favor in the eyes of the Lord. This is the account of Noah. *Noah was a righteous man, blameless among the people of his time.* (Gen. 6:8–9 NIV emphasis added)

The generation in which Noah was declared a "righteous man" was the same generation in which "all humanity" had lost their way—"their true direction." And as the story of Noah's actions after the Flood makes clear, he did not escape the world's debasing influence. It is a testimony to the goodness and mercy of God, not to the goodness of Noah, that he was saved from the waters of the Flood. Noah's effort to follow a higher standard of behavior than his neighbors was counted for "righteousness" and was rewarded by God. But that higher standard was relative.

The idea of being *relatively* righteous—of being the best in a situation where the best is none too good—is repeated elsewhere in the Scriptures. In an incident that takes place many generations after Noah's time, God tells the Hebrew people it is not because of their righteousness that they are being allowed to enter the promised land of Canaan:

> It is not because of your righteousness or your integrity that you are going in to take possession of their land; but on account of the wickedness of those nations. (Deut. 9:5)

The above-quoted Scripture was given after the forty years of wandering in the wilderness. But God's preservation of them during that time was no reason for the Israelites to be lulled into a false sense of security. Like Noah, those who survived in the wilderness were good only relative to the wickedness of other people. Noah's behavior was acceptable only in comparison with the utterly depraved behavior of his neighbors.

Those whom God saved from the forty days of rain were the survivors of a human race which had so corrupted itself that it could no longer live up to its former standards of behavior. The violence to which the creatures of earth had conditioned themselves had caused their regression. The results of that regression are detailed in Genesis 6:11–12. And these details give the reason for the repetitiveness of the covenant story. God cared so much for the animals that he entered into the same covenant relationship with them as He did with human beings. It was necessary to repeat that information so many times because humans had regressed to the point where they would abuse animals and use them in unnatural ways.

This nadir of human development is spelled out in the Bible. God tells Noah and his sons:

> And the fear of you and the dread of you shall be upon every beast of the earth, and upon every fowl of the air, upon all that moveth upon the earth, and upon all the fishes of the sea; into your hand they are delivered. Everything that liveth shall be meat for you; even as the green herb, *have I given* you all things. (Gen. 9:2–3 emphasis added)

The words *have I given* in the above-quoted scripture, should read *have I made*. "Even as the green herb, *have I made* all things." That is the way this particular phrase is translated in other parts of the Bible, and in this instance it would make it clear that God is not "giving" His creatures to human beings for food. Rather, the Bible is reiterating that the Lord "made" all things; the green herbs of the fields as well as all living creatures.

This verse of scripture is a statement of fact: human beings will consume the flesh of other creatures. But along with a misleading translation, human chauvinism has prompted scholars to claim that it constitutes God's blessing on man turned carnivore. But the passage does not signify divine approval of what has taken place. It is not approval—it is acceptance of what has already happened. Just as the Lord accepted that Adam and Eve chose to "know" evil and consequently were unsuited for life in Eden, He now accepted that man—and other creatures—had regressed to feeding on each other's flesh. And although the Bible does not tell us at what point various species made this adaptation, it had taken place by the time of the Flood, when the world had become "degenerate, debased, and vicious."

By Noah's day, many of earth's creatures had changed from herbivorous to carnivorous organisms although God had created all His creatures to be nurtured only by the produce of the earth. The restriction to plants as their only legitimate food immediately followed the appointment of humans as caretakers for God's other creatures. Yet men claim that dominion equals carnivorism. This is a direct contradiction of the Bible:

> God said unto them . . . have dominion over the fish of the sea, and over the fowl of the air, and over every living thing that moveth upon the earth. And God said, "Behold, I have given you every herb bearing seed which is upon the face of all the earth, and every tree, in which is the fruit of a tree yielding seed; to you it shall be for meat." (Gen. 1:28–29)

The restriction to a vegetarian diet as the only legitimate form of food was the standard to which all of earth's creatures had been held from the beginning of time. But during the millennia that had passed since then, human beings had become conditioned—and adapted—to a much lower form of life. Noah and his family, like the people among whom they lived, had become carnivorous. And human development had reached such a nadir that the survivors of the Flood could no longer be held to former standards of behavior. Thus God's mercy kept pace with mankind's regression.

Human understanding had darkened to the point where it could no longer comprehend the higher level on which it had once lived. There were still some food restrictions, however, that human beings had to observe:

> You must not eat meat that has its lifeblood still in it. (Gen. 9:4 NIV)

This verse of Scripture has given rise to many religious regulations that developed around the slaughter of animals. Whether or not an animal's body still had blood in it became a matter of ritual cleanliness. But the point of the Scripture is not a concern with whether or not the carcass had blood in it. The meaning is much more primitive and direct: Human beings were being forbidden to eat creatures that were still alive.

In a regressed world, some animal species were allowed even that. But for human beings this was an ultimate taboo. Unlike animals who devoured their still-struggling prey, humans had to be sure what they ate was dead. Other translations of the Bible make the point clearly:

You must not eat flesh with life . . . JB

You shall not eat flesh with its life . . . NAS

But you must not eat the flesh with the life . . . NEB

The fact that ancient peoples equated life with blood was a safeguard against a gradual slackening of this food taboo. The blood/life belief spawned religious rituals that ensured no blood was left in meat that was to be consumed. Draining the blood ensured that the animal was dead. Without this safeguard, the taboo against eating living flesh probably would have eroded over a period of time, and human beings would have regressed even further.

Homo sapiens was not a species that simply continued on after the Flood. Human beings had gone far backward in the framework of time and space. Instead of the balance of nature that had originally provided food for all creatures from the bounty of the earth, there was now a debased system in which every creature could be the prey of another. And the scriptural prophecy that animals would come to "fear and dread" human beings also came true for other humans. People would prey upon their own species; the powerful would consume the lives and substance of the less powerful—human or animal.

Chapter Four
Abraham and Beyond

Part One: The Patriarch

AFTER THE TIME OF NOAH THERE WAS A LONG period during which there is no biblical report of God's special dealings with an individual. That hiatus begins in prehistorical times and does not end until circa 2000 B.C. The long silence ends with the story of Sarah and Abraham, founding parents of Judaism. The biblical account of their lives and loves gives many clues regarding the kind of development that had been taking place since the time of the Flood.

The information given indicates that human understanding had remained darkened and violence had continued unabated. Abraham's attempt to sacrifice his son Isaac shows this trend clearly. In Abraham's day, human sacrifice had become an acceptable way of worshipping God. Because it was acceptable, the patriarch could set out to Moriah fully expecting to murder his son there.

Theologians have so admired Abraham's obedience in trying to carry out the sacrifice he thought God was demanding that they have ignored a critical issue in the story. This account of Isaac's near-death is pointing out that at its very inception, Judaism chose a higher path than contemporary religions: It substituted animal sacrifice for human sacrifice.

> When they reached the place God had told him about, Abraham built an altar there. . . . He bound his son Isaac and laid him on the altar, on top of the wood. Then he reached out his hand and took the knife to slay his son. But the angel of the Lord called out to him. . . . Do not lay a hand on the boy. . . . Abraham looked up and there in a thicket he saw a ram. . . . He went over and took the ram and sacrificed it as a burnt offering. (Gen. 22:9–13 NAS)

A substitute for Isaac—a ram—appeared at the last minute. This was not to satisfy God's need for sacrifice. It satisfied Abraham's need to sacrifice. The patriarch had gone to Moriah to worship in this way; he would not leave without doing so. To him, such an omission would have represented the worst kind of sacrilege. At this point of human regression, Abraham was incapable of understanding that the sacrifice of any flesh—human or nonhuman—was an abomination to God. It would be many hundreds of years before that message could be communicated by the Latter Prophets.

The human race had fallen so far in its development that it could only begin climbing to its former state a step at a time. In Abraham's day, the crucial first step was the renunciation of human sacrifice. The next step—the rejection of animal sacrifice—would have to come later.

When Abraham took that crucial step of rejecting human sacrifice, he assured his descendants of a pivotal place in God's unfolding plan. Without that rejection, the patriarch and his descendants could not have been the people chosen to represent the spiritual evolution of the human race. Abraham was able to substitute a ram for his son. After that incident it was always understood that the God of Abraham was a God who rejected human sacrifice. Though there would be many times when some of the Israelites would imitate their less-developed neighbors and offer their own children on sacrificial altars, Judaism never required such a sacrifice; it was always understood that human sacrifices were an "abomination" to the God of Israel. But not until the advent of the Latter Prophets did the people begin to accept that the sacrifice of animals was also repugnant in God's sight.

Over a thousand years elapsed between Abraham's rejection of human sacrifice and Isaiah's prophecies against animal sacrifice. During that time, the human race continued its worship of violence and the biblical record of those years presents a near-constant account of human and animal slaughter. But there is a brief respite: The Bible tells of an attempt to condition an entire people to a life that was not violent to either humans or animals. This attempt took place when the Hebrew people wandered for forty years in the wilderness of the Sinai Peninsula.

Part Two: The Wilderness

The children of Israel walked forty years in the wilderness till
all the people that were men of war, which came out of
Egypt, were consumed. (Josh. 5:6 JB)

Under the leadership of Moses, the Hebrew people were
freed from the yoke of Egyptian bondage. Although once
prosperous in Egypt, a time came when they lost all privileges
and power and were reduced to the status of slaves. Finally, in
the midst of their suffering and deprivation, Moses came to lead
them out of Pharaoh's land and begin the journey to Canaan.

The Bible describes Canaan—the Promised Land—as a
place "flowing with milk and honey." The image is pastoral and
nonviolent. This word-picture of a bountiful land is an attempt
to awaken the memory of a paradise now lost. Only in a land
where the inhabitants do not prey on each other could there be
the kind of peaceful cooperation between men and other
creatures that would yield such abundance that it would seem
to be "flowing with milk and honey."

This image of bountiful nourishment that did not
necessitate the slaughter of any creature was presented to a
people accustomed to eating flesh—a people who equated the
eating of meat with being well fed. Only a few months after they
were freed from Egyptian slavery, one of the people's chief
complaints was that they missed the "flesh pots" of Egypt.
Specifically, they bemoaned the lack of meat—something they
had enjoyed even as slaves. In fact, their desire for this kind of
food became so strong that the Hebrews declared they were
better off in Egypt because there, at least, they were given flesh
to eat. (Num. 11:18)

32

In the first months of their wilderness journey, when the conditioning to such food was still strong among the people, they had been provided with the meat they demanded. (Exod. 16:12) But later, when they had been weaned from such a diet by years of eating the manna that God provided, such demands were not acceptable. (Num. 11:4–34)

The years of being sustained in the desert by manna were also years during which all the "men of war" perished. The violence of war and the violence of animal slaughter were in abeyance for most of the wilderness years. But the experiment in nonviolent living failed. When the forty years were over and the Hebrews were ready to enter the Promised Land, the people once again began eating flesh, and the manna no longer fell from heaven.

The Bible gives an account of the way in which the Israelites entered Jericho. No weapons of war were used to penetrate the walls of that Canaanite city. Instead, the sons of Israel marched around the city in a prescribed ritual for seven days. Then the trumpets were sounded, the people shouted, and the walls collapsed. (Josh. 6:20) It was a unique method of entry for a people among whom all the "men of war" had died. No one was killed in the attempt to breach the walls; but after the city fell, the time of nonviolence was over. The Israelites entered the town and proceeded to slaughter all the inhabitants as easily as any seasoned warriors could have done: "They destroyed with the sword every living thing in it—men and women, young and old, cattle, sheep and donkey." (Josh. 6:21)

Once again human beings and animals suffered the same fate: All were slaughtered in the takeover. And the Bible records that man's violence in the land continued unabated—and undenounced—for more than 500 years. During those centuries neither priest nor prophet raised a voice to protest either the human or the animal slaughter that was carried out in the name of the Lord. Instead, the priests taught that such slaughter glorified God.

But eventually the Latter Prophets intruded on this sanctification of violence. It was Jeremiah who denounced the massacre that had taken place when the Hebrews entered Jericho. Speaking in the name of God he told the people that the wholesale slaughter that had taken place when their ancestors entered Canaan had been an abomination in the sight of God—not something to be celebrated:

> I brought you into a fruitful land to enjoy its fruit and the goodness of it, but when you entered upon it you defiled it and made the home I gave you loathsome. (Jer. 2:7 JB)

Denunciations like this had not been heard in Israel. To the contrary, violence in the name of God had become an integral part of religious practices. The victories that resulted in the slaughter of human enemies were celebrated with the slaughter of animals; their blood was endlessly poured over Yahweh's altars as thanksgiving for past triumphs or inducements for future victories. Such mayhem was accompanied by prayers and petitions. Numerous blessings and rituals were developed to sanctify the slaughters that took place on the altars of war as well as on the altars of the Temple.

Ultimately, the sacrificial and ceremonial aspects of religious worship became so firmly entrenched in Judaism that those rituals became totally identified with the worship of God. This was the false worship—the false religion—from which the Latter Prophets called the people to repent. Their insistence that ceremony and sacrifice give way to social justice and nonviolence characterized the epoch of the great prophets of Israel.

For two hundred years their prophetic warnings were heard. But during those centuries there were periods of great prosperity for Judaism; although the people were warned that their violence and selfishness were sowing the seeds of destruction in their own land, a prosperous and powerful nation saw no reason to change. The Temple remained the center of sacrifice, while the poor continued to be exploited by the wealthy.

Then, history intervened.

Chapter Five
Postexilic Judaism

I N 587 B.C. JERUSALEM FELL TO THE BABYLONIAN army. The Temple was destroyed and the Jewish people were exiled to the land of their conquerors. The Babylonian exile lasted fifty years. During those years no animals could be slaughtered on the Temple altars, so instead of sacrificial worship, the people began to form synagogues. In such places, they and their descendants would gather together in the name of the Lord for thousands of years to come.

Eventually, the Babylonians themselves were defeated by the Persians. It was a propitious victory as far as the Hebrews were concerned. Cyrus, king of Persia, was very favorably disposed toward the Jews, and he allowed those who so desired to return to Jerusalem. One of the first things the returnees did was to reinstate sacrificial worship.

Under the supervision of the priests and other leaders, the people built altars and once again slaughtered animals to please

God. The prophets who had denounced the cult of sacrifice were all dead, but the priests were alive and well. They told the people that if they did not offer sacrifices, God would not give His blessing nor withhold His wrath. The book of Ezra records the success of the priesthood in reestablishing the cult of Temple sacrifice:

> When the seventh month came and the Israelites had settled in their towns, the people assembled as one man in Jerusalem. Then Jeshua, son of Jozadak and his fellow priests . . . began to build the altar of the God of Israel to sacrifice burnt offerings on it, in accordance with what is written in the Law of Moses, the man of God . . . they built the altar on its foundations and sacrificed burnt offerings on it to the Lord, both the morning and evening sacrifices. . . . After that they presented the regular burnt offerings, the New Moon sacrifices and the sacrifices for all the appointed sacred feasts of the Lord. (Ezra 3:1–3, 5 NIV)

. The resumption of New Moon sacrifices and other murderous rituals, were a direct refutation of Isaiah's oracle:

> "The multitude of your sacrifices—what are they to me? . . . Your hands are full of blood. . . . Take your evil deeds out of my sight." (Isa. 1:11, 15–16 NIV)

In resuming sacrifice, the Jewish people had reached a milestone on their spiritual journey. This choice had enormous repercussions on their subsequent history. The centrality of Temple worship gave the priests enormous power. By the fourth century B.C, the high priest—like a medieval pope—combined the power of his religious office with the power of a secular prince.

In the centuries that followed, the sacrificial cult flourished. But the prophets had warned of the link between the violence of slaying animals on the altars of God and the violence of slaying human beings in war. Their prophecies proved true. For 500 years the Jewish people slaughtered, or were themselves slaughtered, in the endless power struggles that centered on Palestine. The blood of sacrificial victims ran deep in the House of God while the blood of war victims ran deep in the streets beyond the Temple walls.

During that period various empires ruled the land. Persian, Macedonian, Ptolemaic, Selucid, Jewish, and Roman rulers quickly succeeded each other. Alliances with various powers were made and broken. Finally the Jewish people became embroiled in a brutal civil war in which Pharisee and Saducee tortured and killed each other as mercilessly as any outsider would have done.[1]

Although the Pharisees and Saducees were often on a murderous collision course, their fratricidal slayings of each other did not undermine the power of Temple worship. Ritual slaughter and ceremonial offerings continued unabated. Their continuance was guaranteed by a decision reached by the religious leadership. Henceforth, no individual who claimed to speak in the name of God was to be accepted as God's spokesman. By 200 B.C. it was official: The Age of Prophecy was over. The word of the Lord would now be disseminated only through established religious channels.

The postprophetic age had begun. No longer would the voices of men like Isaiah and Jeremiah be raised in protest against their own priests and political leaders. The words of those great men, now long dead, were safely enshrined in the

Scriptures. There they could be revered, studied—and never put into practice.

But in spite of the fact that the Age of Prophecy had been declared dead two hundred years earlier, the voice of John the Baptist began to be heard in the wilderness of Judea. The people flocked to hear his message. John saw himself in the tradition of the Latter Prophets; he identified himself and his ministry by quoting Isaiah 40:3:

> I am as Isaiah prophesied: A voice that cries in the wilderness, make straight a way for the Lord. (John 1:23)

John's message to his people was, "Repent, for the Kingdom of Heaven is near." (Matt. 3:2) Though he was the son of a priest of Israel, the Baptist warned that claims of a specific religious heritage or belief were of no avail in the sight of God; the Lord demanded something other than traditional claims and traditional forms of worship. And when the powerful and pious Saducees and Pharisees came to investigate this prophet whose fame was spreading all over Palestine, John addressed them as "you brood of vipers." He continued to remain unimpressed by the religious leaders of his day.

Like the prophets who preceded him, John warned his generation that their religious observances were not pleasing to God. He told the people that their judaic heritage did not guarantee their righteousness; being a descendant of the patriarch Abraham was not a guarantee of God's favor. "Produce fruit in keeping with repentance," John said, "and do not begin to say to yourselves, 'We have Abraham for our father.' " (Luke 3:8)

John's popularity became so great that the people thought he might be the anointed one—the Messiah who would lead them into a victorious new era. But the Baptist rejected that idea. Instead, he witnessed to another man—to someone else who would come and reveal what God desired of his people. The one to whom John gave witness was his cousin, Jesus of Nazareth.

---

1. Flavius Josephus. *Wars of the Jews* (Grand Rapids: Kregel Publications, 1978),1.4.1–6.

Chapter Six
Jesus, the Christ

JESUS DID NOT DERIVE HIS SUPPORT FROM THE religious leaders of his day. He never moved in the cliques of power and intrigue that surrounded the priesthood and he was always unpopular within the circles of self-regard that surrounded the pious Pharisees. Neither did the family into which he was born confer any power or prestige. His mother, Mary, was a Jewish girl of modest origins and Joseph, her husband, was a carpenter who plied his trade in the hill country of Galilee, at Nazareth.

But Jesus was not born at Nazareth. When the time for her delivery was at hand, Mary was far south, in the city of Bethlehem. Those who later became disciples of Christ understood his birthplace to be a fulfillment of the prophesy of Micah 5:2:

. . . you Bethlehem, out of you will come for men one who
will be ruler over Israel, whose origins are from of old, from
ancient times. (Matt. 2:6)

This prophecy was quoted in the New Testament, in the
gospel of Matthew, because those who followed Christ
understood that, like the prophets who had spoken before him,
Jesus would teach truths from "of old, from ancient times."
They were the truths that echoed the creation account of
Genesis. Even the birth of Christ was a restatement of the
creation story. In the biblical account, the animals were created
first; man was later set in their midst as caregiver. And the story
of the birth of Jesus tells how the infant was born into a place
that had first sheltered and nurtured animals:

The time came for the baby to be born. . . . She wrapped him
in cloths and placed him in a manger because there was no
room for them in the inn. (Luke 2:6–7)

This theme of human/animal relatedness continues on in
the Nativity story. Luke's gospel tells how the Angel of the Lord
announced the birth of Christ to men who were out in the
fields, caring for their animals:

And there were shepherds living out in the fields nearby,
keeping watch over their flocks at night. An angel of the Lord
appeared to them. "Do not be afraid . . . I bring you good
news. . . . This will be a sign to you; you will find a baby
wrapped in cloths and lying in a manger." (Luke 2:8–10, 12
NIV)

So it was that those chosen to be first to know the good
news of Christ's coming were men who cared for animals. They
were the nurturing caregivers that God had meant man to be

when Adam was placed in Eden. These shepherds were living in a way that, in their time, most closely approximated the peaceful accord between animals and men that God had ordained and the prophets had described in their millennial visions.

The work of the shepherds who attended Jesus at his birth was the antithesis of those whose work centered around the holocaust of animals on the altars at Jerusalem. And Jesus, who was welcomed into the world by men who protected and cared for animals, never participated in the sacrificial rites of the Temple. Neither did his disciples. Just as the beginning of Judaism was marked by the rejection of human sacrifice, so the beginning of Christianity was marked by the rejection of animal sacrifice. It was a fulfillment of the call for reform that had been given by the prophets hundreds of years earlier.

But in spite of the fact that the rejection of animal sacrifice was a critical step forward in the spiritual evolution of the human race, the original followers of Jesus paid little attention to his crucial role in this development. His disciples were more concerned with his appearance as the anointed one—the Christ. In some instances, however, they did record the Master's quotation of the prophet Hosea: "I will have mercy, not sacrifice; knowledge of God, not holocausts." (Hos. 6:6) The gospel of Matthew reports two occasions on which Jesus reminded the people that Hosea had called for an end to sacrificial worship— a call that was still being ignored (see Matt. 9:13, 12:7). But it is the gospel of John that deals at greater length with the matter of Temple sacrifice.

In the fourth chapter of John's gospel there is a report of an incident that took place when Christ was in Samaria. Although of Jewish descent, the Samaritans had long intermarried with other groups, and for many centuries the full-blooded Jewish people had looked down on them. They did not consider the Samaritans to be numbered among the Chosen People. Consequently, the Samaritans had built a temple of their own, at Mt. Gerizim, where they worshipped the God of Israel. They had offered sacrifices and holocausts there until a bloody battle in 128 B.C., during which the Hebrews destroyed the rival temple.

A hundred and fifty years after that destruction, John reports that Jesus stood talking to a woman of Samaria. She pointed out that her ancestors had offered sacrifices at their own temple, but that the Jewish people never accepted those sacrifices as legitimate worship: They claimed that God only accepted the sacrifices made at the Jerusalem Temple.

"Sir," the woman said to Jesus, "I can see that you are a prophet. Our fathers worshipped on this mountain, but you Jews claim the place where we must worship is in Jerusalem." (John 4:19–20 NIV) It was not an idle comment. The claim to a legitimate site for sacrificial worship was not just a matter for debate; the blood of many Samaritans and Jews had been shed over the issue. But challenged by the woman regarding the proper place for such worship, Jesus told her there was no legitimate place to offer animal sacrifices; that such worship was, in itself, antithetical to the worship of God:

> Believe me woman, a time is coming when you will worship the Father neither on this mountain nor in Jerusalem. You Samaritans worship what you do not know; we worship what we do know, for salvation is from the Jews. Yet a time is coming and has now come when the true worshippers will worship the Father in spirit and truth, for they are the kind of worshippers the Father seeks. God is spirit and his

worshippers must worship in spirit and in truth. (John 4:21–24 NIV)

In his declaration, "salvation is from the Jews," Jesus was referring to the continuity of revelation among the Jewish people; a continuing record of their spiritual journey that was preserved in their scriptures. It was a record that showed the Spirit of God repeatedly trying to lead the human race back into the light of understanding that it had possessed at the Creation. It was also a record of the human refusal to walk in that light.

In his declaration to the Samaritan woman, Jesus was also prophesying the imminent destruction of the Temple where animal sacrifices took place. For many centuries the Jewish people had ignored prophetic warnings to end their sacrificial worship. Now, the cult was about to end. In A.D. 70, fewer than forty years after Jesus announced its ruin, the Temple at Jerusalem was destroyed. Since it was the only place where victims could be offered to God, its destruction signaled the end of sacrificial worship in Judaism. And from that time to this, no animals have been slaughtered on the altars of the God of Israel. But up to the time that the Temple was destroyed, the cult of sacrifice continued to thrive.

In predicting an end to this bloody worship, Jesus was continuing the revelation of the Latter Prophets: God was a loving parent who cared for all creation—human and nonhuman. Even that which seemed of little worth in human eyes was of value in the sight of God:

> Are not five sparrows sold for two pennies? And [yet] not one
> of them is forgotten or uncared for in the presence of God.
> (Luke 12:6 AMP)

47

Jesus continually revealed a God of compassion whose concern extended to all creatures. And it was the slaughter of animals, in the name of God, that led him to the only aggressive confrontation reported of his ministry. That confrontation took place at the Jerusalem Temple where Christ took direct action against the evils of sacrifice. He freed those animals who were about to be slaughtered and disrupted the entire procedure that surrounded the sacrificial rites:

> When it was almost time for the Jewish Passover, Jesus went up to Jerusalem. In the Temple courts he found men selling cattle, sheep and doves, and others sitting at tables exchanging money. So he made a whip out of cords and drove all from the Temple area, both sheep and cattle; he scattered the coins of the money changers and overturned their tables. To those who sold doves he said, Get these out of here! How dare you turn my Father's house into a market? (John 2:13–16 NIV)

The Synoptic Gospels (Matthew, Mark, and Luke) as well as the gospel of John, record this event. It is the only time that Jesus is reported to have committed an aggressive act. And it was the slaughter of animals, in the name of God, that led to this uncharacteristic action.

Most Christians know about this incident, which is euphemistically called "the cleansing of the Temple." But few realize that it is the pivotal event of Holy Week. It set in motion the arrest, trial, and death of Jesus because in trying to end the slaughter of animals, he was attacking the economic foundation of Jerusalem. The Holy City had become the center of sacrificial religion 600 years earlier when the Temple there had been declared the only legitimate place for sacrifice.

The entire city and its inhabitants were dependent upon the Temple for their survival. Laborers, artisans, craftsmen, and farmers were as committed to the maintenance of the sacrificial cult as were the priests, Levites, and others directly involved in its daily activities. In modern terms, ancient Jerusalem would be classified as a tourist-dependent city.

There were always many pilgrims in the Holy City and three times a year, during the major religious observances of Judaism, the many became a multitude. And never more so than during Passover. Because such great crowds would be gathered in Jerusalem, it was the perfect time for Jesus to carry out his assault on the sacrificial system. Not only would there be many witnesses to what he did, thousands more would hear about it as the story of what took place was passed around among the pilgrims lodged in and around the city.

Mark's gospel makes it clear that the attack on the sacrificial system was a planned event, not an impulsive act. After describing the triumphal entry into the Holy City when the crowds called "Hosanna," his gospel reports that:

> Jesus entered Jerusalem and went to the Temple. *He looked around at everything, but since it was already late, he went on to Bethany with the twelve.* (Mark 11:11 emphasis added.)

The action Jesus planned was to be a very public spectacle, but by the time he had gotten past the cheering crowds who thronged the entry road to Jerusalem, most people had returned to their homes or to the overcrowded inns that housed them during the Passover season. So he went on to Bethany, where he would spend the night at the home of Lazarus.

But before Jesus left the city for the night, when he "looked around at everything" he would have seen the animals who were jammed into the Temple enclosure. The next day was the 10th of Nisan, the traditional day that the male head of the household picked out the animal who would be killed—in honor of its Creator.

The victim was chosen according to a strict protocol: the number of people eating together dictated the size of the animal they could eat. But the animal purchased on the 10th of Nisan would not be killed until the 14th—the eve of Passover. Because each man killed his own animal at this season, the number of sacrificers and the number of their victims was so great that the purchase and the killing could be not carried out on the same day.

From ancient records, scholars have reconstructed the events that took place on the day of sacrifice. The killing began at 3:00 p.m. and by sundown about 18,000 animals would be dead. Because the Temple could not accommodate all the "worshippers" at the same time, the victims had to be killed in three shifts.

Approximately 6,000 people comprised each shift and, since the sacrifice was a yearling, the men usually carried the lambs on their shoulders. Once in the place of slaughter, they lined up in long rows next to a row of priests. The shofar would sound and the men would wrest the lambs to the ground, slitting their throats. As they bled to death, the priests standing next to them would catch the blood in large buckets. When these were full they would be passed up the line to those who stood by the altar, they would throw the blood against the side of the altar. The empty buckets would be recycled and refilled with the blood of more lambs. .

Although it was set up efficiently, neither the human nor the nonhuman creatures who were part of the slaughter process always behaved efficiently. Sometimes the knife was not sharp enough, or the lamb struggled too hard, and although the blood started to flow from its throat, a frantic yearling had to be wrestled into submission before a better cut could be made.

Of course the slaughtered animals lost all control of their bladders and kidneys. The smells, the frenzy of the dying creatures, and the endless buckets of blood thrown on the altar in the name of God, make it obvious that this ritual of terror and violence was the worship of an idol. This god-of-the-slaughter was created by human beings in their own, fallen image.

Because this slaughter of the innocent was idolatrous worship, Isaiah and the other Latter Prophets had called for the end of sacrificial religion. But they had not taken action against the Temple cult. Now, hundreds of years later, Jesus Christ, who began his ministry claiming to be the fulfillment of Isaiah's prophecy (Luke 4:16–20) took action against that system.

Preaching against the religious establishment was one thing; trying to overthrow the sacrificial system which was its foundation, was another. After he did that, nothing would be forgiven him. Jesus disrupted the Temple worship on the 10th of Nisan. By the 14th, he was dead. Like the innocent animals he tried to free he, too, was killed—in the name of God.

Because his freeing of the animals is the only incident recorded in the Bible of Jesus taking direct action against the system, it makes a powerful statement regarding his opposition to sacrificial worship. But because Christian exegetes have paid little attention to the Old Testament condemnation of animal sacrifice—either ignoring or rationalizing it—they have lacked any sense of the profanity that its continuation represented to

Jesus. Consequently, the theories they have offered for his uncharacteristic action have totally missed the mark.

The usual explanation is that Christ was angry because the money changers were cheating the people. Alternatively, it is said that the preslaughter procedures at the Temple had become "too commercial." But there are no biblical or extra-biblical facts on which to base such theories. The Bible does not say that people were being cheated; and providing coins for the purchase of animals was a necessary part of the sacrificial system. From all accounts Jesus was never overly concerned with the monetary practices of his time. (See Matt. 22:17–21.) He even had a tax collector among his disciples at a time when these men were detested by the Jewish people.

In refusing to acknowledge the importance that Israel's prophets gave to the abolition of sacrifices, traditional Christianity has followed the footsteps of Orthodox Judaism. After the era of the Latter Prophets, the Hebrews rebuilt their altars and reinstituted animal sacrifice. And after the death of Jesus, Christianity reinstituted the value of sacrifice by claiming that the God who could not be appeased by the perpetual slaughter of animals was finally appeased by the sacrifice of His son. In both instances, the idea that slaughter is pleasing to God was reestablished.

This allowed human beings to continue to project upon God their own appetite for vengeance and violence. Again and again, they have insisted on portraying God as One who demanded the death of helpless creatures to appease His anger or to assuage His sense of "justice."

Yet the Scriptures continue to witness to a God whose nature precludes such violence. They tell of a Creator whose love and compassion extends to all creatures.

In the tradition of the Latter Prophets, Jesus described God as a loving parent, One who "causes his sun to rise on the evil and the good." Christ urged his followers to demonstrate the same goodness to all creatures—even to those whom they considered their enemies. The word "enemy" had too long been an excuse for murder and mayhem:

> You have heard it was said, Love your neighbor and hate your enemy. But I tell you, Love your enemies and pray for those who persecute you that you may be the sons of your Father in Heaven. He causes his sun to rise on the evil and the good and sends rain on the righteous and the unrighteous. (Matt. 5:43–45 NIV)

Jesus described his own ministry as one of caring for others, and he often referred to animals to make this point. In so doing, he was testifying to the ability of nonhuman creatures to demonstrate characteristics of love and concern. In the gospel of Matthew, Christ likened his desire to protect and care for his people to the desire of a mother hen to care for her young:

> O, Jerusalem, Jerusalem . . . how often I have longed to gather your children together as a hen gathers her chicks under her wings, but you would not. (Matt. 23:37)

More often, Jesus used the behavior of lambs to make his point. He likened his own role to that of the caregiving shepherd. In John's gospel he refers to himself by a title that has remained through the ages: Jesus designated himself "The Good Shepherd." (John 10:14)

Just as the shepherds who were caring for their flocks around Bethlehem played an important part at the birth of Christ, so the relationship between shepherd and sheep played an important part in his adult life. Jesus frequently likened that relationship to his own calling. In so doing, he was continuing in the tradition of the prophet Isaiah, who had used the same idea to express God's loving care for all creation:

> Here is your God. . . . He tends his flock like a shepherd: He gathers the lambs in his arms and carries them close to his heart; he gently leads those that have young. (Isa. 40:9, 11 NIV)

Jesus used these images as symbols of God's relatedness to human beings, but he was also reminding people that an ideal relationship with animals was one in which they were the object of man's concern and care. The life of the shepherd was a life of human service to nonhuman creatures. It was a lifestyle that Jesus consistently held up as a model to his followers.

Despite God's having ordained men to care for animals, and despite the prophets' denunciations of sacrificial worship, the slaughter had continued. In biblical times, lambs were most frequently sacrificed. Their gentleness made them the ideal victims. Neither priest nor penitent were endangered by the frenzied and dangerous struggles of a creature faced with death. Consequently, sheep were endlessly slaughtered as atonements for sin, as thanksgiving offerings, and as redemptors for more valuable animals.

The nonviolent nature of the lamb being led to slaughter was also a basis for the designation of Jesus as "the Lamb of God." Like the lamb, Christ did not attempt to inflict violence on those who wanted to kill him. When the authorities came to arrest him in Gethsemane, he ordered his followers to refrain from retaliation. And when one of his disciples attacked and wounded a man, Jesus ordered him to sheath his weapon: "Put your sword back," he said, "for all who draw the sword will die by the sword." (Matt. 26:52)

Refusing to meet violence with violence, Jesus went to his death "like a sheep that is led to the slaughterhouse." (Acts 8:32)

Years before it took place, John the Baptist had predicted Christ's manner of death. When Jesus first began his ministry, the Baptist had called out regarding him, "Behold the Lamb of God." (John 1:29) And after his death the disciples of Jesus continued to identify him with the animals he had so often referred to during his life. "The Good Shepherd" had become the "Lamb of God." Just as animals were sacrificed because men said this was pleasing to God, so Jesus of Nazareth—said to be a blasphemer—was slain because men thought this would be pleasing to God.

Chapter Seven
The Book of Revelation:
The Life to Come

THE IDENTIFICATION OF CHRIST WITH THE ANIMAL kingdom is continued in the Book of Revelation. That book tells of things that are to come and is the record of a vision given to John, a disciple of Jesus, a few decades after the crucifixion. In that vision the "Lamb" has a pivotal role. John's vision told of an afterlife—of another kind of existence—wherein happiness would be unmarred because "God shall wipe away all tears." (Rev. 21:4)

For almost 2,000 years countless women and men have clung to a hope of the kind of afterlife recorded in Revelation. They have held this hope for themselves and for their loved ones.

John's revelation has continued to play a crucial role in giving hope to human hearts. Although his vision did not give an answer to why life holds so much pain and misery, it did promise that such suffering would end. The Book of Revelation promises that there will be a new heaven and a new earth in which "there shall be no more death, neither sorrow, nor crying, neither shall there be anymore pain; for the former things are passed away." (Rev. 21:4)

Revelation also tells of a time when human beings will gather around the throne of God. There they will sing songs of praise and joy. And John's vision tells something more about that heavenly existence: It reveals that God's other creatures—the animals—will join in that heavenly chorus. (See chapters four and five of Revelation.)

John's prophetic vision of an afterlife that includes animals was a continuation—and a completion—of the message given by the Latter Prophets. Those men had begun the task of bringing to consciousness the fact that nonhuman creatures were of great value in God's sight: The prophets foretold a world in which animals, as well as humans, would exist in peace and contentment. These prophets taught that when human beings had ceased their violence, the violence of animals would also be a thing of the past. Then, together, animals and humans would enjoy the blessed existence of a restored creation: The lion and the lamb will lie down together and a little child will lead them.

But although the Scriptures repeatedly witness to the high value that the Creator places on animal life, human beings have been reluctant to accept that truth. They have been aided and abetted in that reluctance by biblical scholars. Prompted by human chauvinism, many scholars have gone to great lengths to obfuscate the scriptural message of animal worth and animal afterlife. To do this, they have misused the tools of exegesis, symbolism, and translation. Nowhere is this misuse more apparent than in the Book of Revelation.

Although Revelation is replete with signs and symbols, it also deals with eternal realities. And the existence of so many symbolic passages has never caused humans to doubt the book's promise of their own redemption and restoration. When John's vision describes people enjoying the presence of the Creator in heavenly places, no scholars find this scenario unreasonable; neither do they consider this too high an honor for human beings. But when the same passages of Scripture tell of the presence of animals in the same high places, scholars decided that the Bible really couldn't mean what it said: Surely animals are not worthy of such honor.

The first official refusal to believe what the Scriptures said came about a hundred years after John's vision had been recorded. At that time, Ireneus, the bishop of Lyons, decided that passages telling of animals present in heaven didn't really mean what they said. He decided that the four animals Revelation described as being gathered around the throne of God couldn't really be symbols of animal creation. The bishop decided they were actually men—in disguise. He also decided that these men-disguised-as-animals were specific persons: namely, Matthew, Mark, Luke, and John, the Four Evangelists.

The biblical passages on which he based his conclusions are quoted below. They provide testimony to the bishop's original thinking rather than to his scriptural fidelity:

> Then, in my vision, I saw a door open in heaven and heard the same voice speaking to me. . . . Come up here: I will show you what is to come in the future. With that, the Spirit possessed me and I saw a throne standing in heaven, and the One who was sitting on the throne. . . . Around the throne in

a circle . . . I saw twenty-four elders sitting. . . . In the center, grouped around the throne itself, were four animals with many eyes, in front and behind. The first animal was like a lion, the second like a bull, the third animal had a human face, and the fourth animal was like a flying eagle. . . . Every time the animals glorified and honored and gave thanks to the One sitting on the throne, who lives for ever and ever, the twenty-four elders prostrated themselves before him to worship the One who lives for ever and ever. . . . (Rev. 4:1–2, 4, 6–7, 9–10 JB)

Despite the chauvinism that prompted Ireneus and his successors to reject the scriptural references to animals in heaven, there are scholarly works that give accurate information. These works note that the four animals described in Revelation 4:7 are representative of nonhuman as well as human creatures. They also note that when the Bible describes these animals as having, respectively, the likenesses of a lion, an ox, an eagle, and a man, it is recording the fact that all kinds of God's creatures are represented in heaven. The four creatures "are the heads of animate creation; the lion of wild beasts, the ox of tame beasts, the eagle of birds; the man of all (mankind)."[1]

There are other reference works that preserve the real meaning of these biblical verses that refer to animals. Unfortunately, they are not generally accessible. But they are accessible to exegetes and translators. Still, these scholars have continued to obscure the Bible's message of animal restoration. And in the twentieth century, it was the translators who were most successful in confusing the issue.

Over the last hundred years, there has been a proliferation of Bible translations. But until recently, the King James version—published in 1611—was the standard Bible for Protestant readers. And, too often, the archaic English of that translation served to confuse rather than clarify the Greek text. This is what happened in the matter of biblical references to animals.

The King James Bible never uses the term *animal*. As far as it is concerned, the word might as well not exist. Instead it uses the word *beast*. And it is used whether the meaning implied is positive, neutral, or pejorative. Consequently, the positive message of Revelation 4:7 that refers to the "four beasts" gathered around the throne of God is juxtaposed to the very negative use of the word when it refers to the dreaded Beast of the Apocalypse: the Beast that wars on God's people.

But although the King James translation did not distinguish between *beast* and *animal*, the Greek language does. And Greek is the language in which the New Testament is written. Modern English makes the same distinction. *Zoon* is the Greek equivalent of the word *animal* and it is used to refer to nonhuman creatures in general. *Therion* is equivalent to the word *beast* and has the same English connotation of a savage and brutish creature.

This equivalent usage of English and Greek would seem to ensure the accurate translation of passages referring to animals. But the use of modern English cannot overcome another obstacle that stands in the way of accurate translation: Too often, the bias of a translator can subtly, or grossly, distort the meaning of a text. This has been especially true of the verses in Revelation that depict animals, as well as humans and angels, enjoying the presence of their Creator.

As long as the archaic language of the King James Bible allowed scholars to read that "beasts" were admitted into the presence of God, it was relatively easy to decide—as Bishop Ireneus had done—that the Scriptures did not really mean what they said. Translators could reason that savage and brutish creatures would hardly be singing God's praises in heavenly places. But this human chauvinism was somewhat shaken when modern scholars were faced with the fact that *zoon* is correctly translated as *animal*—not as *beast*. When the proper translation is made, the negative connotation that the word *beast* has for the modern reader is no longer present.

Because *animal* is a neutral, general term, its use in translation would have made it difficult for scholars to keep insisting that the Bible is referring to four men in disguise when it plainly says four animals.

Several other passages in the Book of Revelation pose a similar threat to human prejudice. Some of those passages mention three different kinds of God's creatures—human, angel, and animal—in the same sentence. This kind of verse makes it even harder to maintain that the animals mentioned are merely symbolic references to men:

> Every time the animals glorified and honored and gave thanks to the One sitting on the throne, who lives for ever and ever, the twenty-four elders prostrated themselves before Him to worship the One. . . . (Rev. 4:9–10 JB)

> And all the angels who were standing in a circle around the throne surrounding the elders and the four animals, prostrated themselves before the throne worshiping God. (Rev. 7:11 JB)

Scripture verses like these challenged the prejudices of some scholars. But they were able to meet the challenge. They did so by totally disregarding the intent of Scripture. They

The Book of Revelation

opted for a legalistic translation that was as misleading as it was dishonest. The word *zoon*—the word that means *animal* in the Greek text—was not translated as *animal*. Instead, it was translated as *living creature*. This translation had a twofold advantage: It was nebulous enough to obscure the biblical message concerning animals, and the definition was "legal."

It was legal because modern American dictionaries define *animal* as anything that is not a plant or as any living organism. But such definitions are general and are inadequate for particular situations. No one trying to communicate a message regarding animals would use the term *living creatures*; to do so would only cause confusion. A sign that said NO LIVING CREATURES ALLOWED would be more confusing than informative. It could be forbidding the entrance of bird, animal, or human being. In the same way, when they translated the Scriptures to read that "living creatures" are grouped around the throne of God, scholars confused the issue and obscured the Bible's specific reference to animals.

Translators were aware of the confusion that their terminology caused, so they took care to ensure that they did not translate *zoon* as *living creature* when such confusion served no purpose. The following verses illustrate this point.

> But these men revile the things they do not understand . . . like unreasoning *animals*. (Jude 1:10 NAS emphasis added)

> For the bodies of those *animals* whose blood is brought into the holy place by the high priest as an offering for sin are burned outside the camp. (Heb. 13:11 NAS emphasis added)

In each of the above verses, the word *zoon* is correctly translated as *animal*. And it is translated this way by the same scholars who substitute the words *living creatures* when they are translating the Book of Revelation.

This scholarly prejudice against translating the Greek text accurately when it says that animals share in an afterlife colored the translation of most modern versions of the Bible. But there is a notable exception: The Jerusalem Bible correctly translates *zoon* as animal—even in the Book of Revelation.

The men who produced this version of the Bible were able to maintain fidelity to the Greek text because their belief system was not threatened by a correct translation. The Jerusalem Bible was produced by Catholic scholars; and their religious tradition long ago settled questions about who or what went to heaven. By contrast, the diversity of Protestant beliefs does not permit a definite repository of doctrine—a *magisterium*—to bolster beliefs. Consequently, when faced with scriptural verses that pictured a human/animal togetherness in heavenly places, Protestant scholars protected their prejudice and their sensibilities. Catholic scholars were already protected against such ideas.

But it is an encouraging sign of the times in Western civilization that such prejudices need protection. Until a century ago, human consciousness had not developed to the point where animal welfare was a matter of wide concern. It was only after the obscenities of slavery and war—often justified by biblical theologians—were seriously questioned that an insight into the evils of animal exploitation began.

---

1. E.W. Bullinger, *A Critical Lexicon and Concordance to the English and Greek New Testament* (Grand Rapids: Zondervan, 1975), p. 147.

Part II: Prologue
The Signs of the Times

"... can ye not discern the signs of the times?" (Matt. 16:3)

THEOLOGIANS OF VARIOUS PERSUASIONS DISCUSS
the necessity of understanding what the "signs of the
times" are saying. By this they mean the ability to relate
the various developments that are taking place in the world to
the ongoing revelation of God. Properly discerned, these signs
can tell us where the Spirit of God is leading.

In the past, practical consideration of basic human needs
kept most people from responding to the fact that the treatment
of animals is unnecessarily cruel and exploitative. The need for
animal skins for bodily protection long co-existed with the
belief that adequate nutrition meant the eating of flesh. And the
need for animals to do the work of farming, building, and
commerce often resulted in their abuse. But in our own day,
various scientific and technological developments have become

"signs of the times": They have removed obstacles that once seemed to stand in the way of the humane treatment of animals. These developments have provided vastly superior alternatives to the use and abuse of animals.

Many countries now have synthetic fabrics available. These materials provide more warmth and protection than animal fur. Lightweight and durable, synthetic products have eliminated the need to hunt, trap, and raise animals for their fur.

The introduction of "horseless carriages" began the widespread development of machinery that farmed, built, and transported the products of commerce more effectively than any work animal could do. This mechanization of labor effectively removed a main cause of animal abuse.

Barely a decade ago, mainstream nutritionists insisted that animal protein was of paramount importance in maintaining optimum health. This claim was bolstered by the constant dissemination of "evidence" that depicted the physiology of human beings as a schematic for carnivorism. That schematic was a misrepresentation of the facts. Today we know that the physiology of human beings—from teeth through arteries to intestines—gives irrefutable evidence that the optimum diet for human beings is not meat. In fact, the ingestion of meat puts an enormous strain on the entire body. And though there is still the attempt to include meat in the diet by decreasing its intake and increasing the ingestion of vegetables and grains, that effort at co-existence is doomed to failure. It is becoming obvious to the health care community that it is not the addition of plant foods to the diet that works seeming miracles; it is the removal of flesh foods that increases people's physical well being.

The science of nutrition, the mechanization of labor, and the availability of synthetic fabrics are all "signs of the times";

they give notice that the age of the unthinking abuse of animals is coming to an end. It is ending because new knowledge and technology have undermined the rationale for such exploitation.

At the same time that technology is providing alternatives to animal-based products, communications between human and nonhuman beings have dramatically increased. In the past, the ability of animals was conveniently underrated, and the affection, loyalty, and intelligence they demonstrated was ignored or mislabeled "instinctive." We know now that their capacity for feeling and for communication is much more extensive and sophisticated than was formerly acknowledged. Pet-companions, for example, are credited with making an important contribution to the physical, mental, and emotional health of their owners. These animals are able to form bonds of empathy and affection because there is an underlying similarity of needs between them and the people with whom they interact.

Animals have also become eyes for the blind and ears for the deaf—trusted companions whose love and service are irreplaceable. Some have shown themselves able and willing to operate sophisticated machines for their paralyzed human companions, making life bearable for those who otherwise might not be able to endure. Through the use of signs, animals have demonstrated the ability to communicate with human beings in a human language.

But at the same time that awareness of the similarities between humans and nonhumans has come to the fore, the brutalization of animals has found new avenues of expression. In laboratories and on campuses all over the world, the most sensitive and intelligent animals are subjected to atrocities.

Labeled "research" by those who perform them, torturous and unnecessary experiments are carried out although alternative methods render experimentation on living animals obsolete.

The refusal of many researchers to utilize available, alternative methods in the laboratory is similar to the refusal of many people to use alternatives to animal products in order to meet their clothing and fashion needs. Even when synthetic fabrics are readily available, there are consumers who still demand the skin, fur, teeth, and tusks of other creatures as decorations for their own bodies or as statements of their affluence. Technology can provide humane alternatives to the exploitation of animals, but society dictates whether or not humane treatment becomes the standard.

The decision to live life with respect and concern for all creatures that inhabit the earth is, first of all, an individual choice. But if the human race is to evolve spiritually and morally, that choice must eventually reflect a societal standard. The Kingdom of God promised by the Bible is a kingdom in which humans and nonhumans must live in peace with their own kind and with all other species. It is the world promised by the prophets, in which "the wolf also shall dwell with the lamb . . . and the calf and the young lion and the fatling together, and a little child shall lead them." (Isa. 11:6)

The Kingdom of God, come to earth, is a kingdom in which justice, compassion, and love for all creatures will be a reality. It is the kind of world Jesus told His followers to expect when He taught them to pray:

> Our Father which art in heaven, Hallowed be Thy name. Thy Kingdom come. Thy will be done, as in heaven, so in earth. (Luke 11:2)

Chapter Eight
Atonement and Dominion

Part One: Atonement

SHORTLY AFTER THE DEATH OF JESUS, SAUL OF Tarsus, a Pharisee committed to the persecution of an embryonic Christianity, had a visionary experience that profoundly affected his own life and the development of Christianity.

He was traveling north on the road from Jerusalem to make an official visit to the synagogues at Damascus. Armed with a letter of authority from the high priest and a contingent of guards, he was intent on making prisoners of any Jews who had become apostates. But somewhere along the road he experienced a blinding light and fell to the ground. He heard a voice saying "Saul, Saul, why persecutest thou me?" The stricken man asked the source of the voice and was told, "I am Jesus whom thou persecutest." (Acts 9:4–5)

The power of this experience changed Saul the Pharisee into Paul the Apostle. The letters he wrote after his conversion comprise the bulk of New Testament scriptures and are foundational in the development of Christian doctrine. And paramount in those epistles are the teachings that later came to be known as the doctrine of the atonement.

For Paul, who claimed to be a Pharisee among Pharisees (Acts 23:6), there was no redemption from the penalty due to sin without the death of a victim. It was this belief that led him to represent the death of Christ as the zenith of sacrificial worship. In the Book of Hebrews he wrote:

> Neither by the blood of goats and calves, but by his own blood he [Christ] entered into the holy place, having obtained eternal redemption for us. For if the blood of bulls and of goats and the ashes of an heifer, sprinkling the unclean, sanctifieth to the purifying of the flesh; how much more shall the blood of Christ. . . . (Heb. 9:12–14)

In the Book of Romans Paul wrote, "[God] spared not his own son, but delivered him up for us all." (Romans 8:32). And he is the author of the passage of Scripture that restates the Levitical pronouncement that "without the shedding of blood, there is no remission [of sins]." This statement, recorded in Hebrews 9:22, has become a Christian mantra repeated endlessly, and mindlessly, through the centuries.

Paul could develop and preach his theory of Christ as the ultimate sacrificial victim only because he never met Jesus. He never walked with the Master as he taught about the nature of God and his own mission on earth. He did not know the parable of the Prodigal Son which Christ used to show that God's love and compassion was ever-present; that forgiveness was not to be bought with the blood of a victim. Neither did he know Jesus taught his followers that by always acting with compassion and mercy they would be demonstrating their kinship with the God who is "kind even unto the unthankful and to the evil. Be ye therefore merciful, as your Father also is merciful." (Luke 6:35–36)

The God whom Jesus came to earth to reveal was nothing like the God of Paul's understanding: A God who needed the sacrifice of countless animals, or of His own son, in order to be reconciled to a sinful humanity. And because Christ had not chosen Paul to be a witness to his earthly ministry, the only other way the man could have known what Jesus taught, and did, was through the witness of the Gospels. But that record had not yet been committed to writing and Paul did not return to Jerusalem and meet with the Apostles of Jesus until almost three years after his conversion. Then after only two weeks, during which time he established his claim as Apostle to the Gentiles, he headed north again. He did not meet with Peter, or the other church elders who had known Jesus, for another ten years.

During those years he continued to construct his own theory of Christ as the sacrificial victim. In order to do this Paul, like his Jewish ancestors and Christian descendants, had to ignore the biblical texts that denounced any kind of sacrifice—animal or human. And although Christianity had no tradition of animal sacrifice to justify, through Paul it retained and built upon the orthodox Jewish insistence that this bloody worship was divinely ordained. Christianity validated the concept of sacrificial religion, and then decreed that the death of Jesus was a sacrifice of such magnitude that it finally satisfied the "justice" of a God who had not been propitiated by the shed blood of countless animals.

In the centuries that followed the writing of Paul's Epistles, various spokesmen built their own theories on the unstable foundation of his conjectures. And early churchmen like Ireneus, Justin, Tertullian, and Augustine presented variations on the theme of Christ's propitiary death, claiming that the sacrifice of animals was the God-ordained prototype of that death.[1]

But unlike Paul, these men had not been conditioned by a religious tradition that had inculcated in them the righteousness of animal sacrifice. And, unlike Paul, they had access to the Gospels. They knew of Jesus' repeated reference to Hosea's oracle, "I will have mercy, not sacrifice, knowledge of God, not holocausts" (Hosea 6:6). And they knew of his attempt to dismantle the sacrificial system—an action that ensured his death. Yet, those early churchmen, like their predecessors and their modern counterparts, seem determined to preserve the concept of a God who demanded the death of His creatures.

The doctrine of the atonement, with its underlying validation of sacrificial religion, continues to be promulgated because it acts as the covering for a multitude of sins. If God demanded the death of countless animals in the service of a righteous goal, then humankind can continue to maim, kill, and consume them in the service of what it claims is a righteous goal: the subjection of all creation to the will of human beings.

Without the validation of a sacrificial religion that deifies the destruction of God's creatures, the claim of human dominion over the earth could not have been interpreted as a license to ravage the planet, and all its creatures.

Without the validation of sacrificial religion, "And God gave dominion over the earth" would be interpreted in the spirit in which it was given: Men and women were given the opportunity to be caretakers—stewards of God's creation.

Part Two: Dominion

Although the Bible has a great deal to say about God's concern for animals, for the most part this subject is ignored. The human bias that sees its own species as having preeminence—dominion—over all other creatures has distorted the biblical message.

This bias continues in spite of the fact that the Scriptures depict the spiritual journey of animals just as surely as they describe the human journey. The Bible traces their story from the time of creation, through their sojourn in a fallen world, to a millennial world they will share with their human companions. And in the Book of Revelation, both wild and domestic animals are shown in heavenly places, praising God for their redemption.[2] It is the creation narrative that gives the reason for this animal presence in heaven; for their immortality.

The Book of Genesis plainly states that animals, like humans, were created as *nefesh chaya*: living souls. (Gen. 1:21, 30) Scholars have obscured this fact by translating the same words differently. When applied to Adam, *nefesh chaya* reads "living soul." (Gen. 2:7) But when the same term is used about animals it is translated as "living creature." (Gen 2:19) And although there is no theological, or biblical basis for their belief, those who want to exercise a ruthless dominion over animals believe that God overlooks the most sadistic and cruel treatment of sentient beings, as long as they do not have a soul. Hence, the centuries-long determination to obscure the biblical news that animals, too, are living souls.

Along with the insistence that animals do not have a soul, the dominion theory relies heavily on the assertion that God specifically created them for man's use. But Scripture refutes this chauvinistic claim. The Bible is very definite about the reason for the creation of the animals. It says that Adam was lonely, and they were created to be his companions. Formed like him from the ground, they were like him in their spiritual essence: They, too, were endowed with God-given souls. (See Gen. 2:7, 19.)

Contrary to popular belief, the Bible does not say that it was Eve who was first created to be a helpmate for Adam. It says that God formed the animals for this purpose:

> The Lord God formed the man of the dust of the ground. . . .
> And the Lord God said, "It is not good that the man should
> be alone; I will make an help meet for him." And out of the
> ground the Lord God formed every beast. (Gen. 2:7, 18–19)

Ultimately it was only Eve, the female counterpart of the male, who could alleviate Adam's loneliness. But the animals continued to be the beloved companions they were created to be—until the Fall.

The Bible also shows that Adam's initial encounter with the animals was a very personal one. "Adam gave names to all [the animals]." (Gen. 2:20) In its use of the word *shem* to describe the process whereby he named the animals, the Hebrew language indicates the uniqueness that characterizes each animal, as well as each person. By definition, *shem* denotes individuality: the same kind of individuality connoted by a person's name. Adam's naming of other creatures was not an impersonal classification of genus or species: It was a personal encounter with individual creatures. It was a recognition that they, like him, were individual beings.

But in the face of all evidence to the contrary, scholars have recently devised another theory to diminish the message of human and animal relatedness. They have decided that in earlier times, those who named others were thought to be exercising power—dominion—over either humans or animals. This self-generated theory has become a staple of conventional, scholarly wisdom although it does not stand up to any objective observation.

Clearly, neither Adam nor Eve would have believed in such power. Adam named Eve but could not control her desire for forbidden fruit. And although they were the ones who gave names to their children, neither Adam nor Eve were able to exercise control over their offspring. Nor were the numerous patriarchs and matriarchs of biblical times able to exercise control over the children, or the animals, they had named.

The development of spurious theories as proof that humans have always exercised a God-given dominion over animals takes its place alongside corrupt biblical exegesis in the effort to preserve the centrality of human existence.

In misrepresenting the Scriptures, biblical exegetes and other scholars encourage the sinfulness of those who want to relegate nonhumans to the category of soulless "things" in order to continue exploiting them. Even the biblically illiterate use these self-serving interpretations to justify the torment and slaughter of an infinite variety of God's creatures. In the pursuit of sportsmanship, of economic gain, and of science, animals are hunted, trapped, and subjected to unspeakable atrocities. And in a Judeo-Christian culture, this evil is excused on the basis of a God-given dominion of the earth.

---

1. Through the centuries, various atonement theories have enjoyed popularity, but whether the theory claims that God sent Jesus into the world in order to be a sacrifice for sin, or alternatively, that Christ offered himself as a sacrifice, the underlying rationale is the same: God is pleased by the slaughter of His creatures.
2. See page 59 onward.

Chapter Nine
Thou Shalt Not Kill

TOO OFTEN, RELIGIOUS DOGMA ECLIPSES OR contradicts the teachings of Christ and the Prophets. Man-made doctrines like the atonement and the dominion theory are used as rationales to maim and kill animals, with a self-righteousness that is impenetrable. This contempt for God's creatures is demonstrated in a variety of ways, among which is the enjoyment of recreational killing.

Unlike other forms of animal exploitation which are indulged by both Jews and Christians, hunting has always been censured by traditional Jewish teaching. Among Christians, however, there is not only an acceptance of recreational killing, it is often a church-sponsored activity. This divergence is a glaring exception to a traditional reliance on Jewish sources and commentaries.

Aside from the identity of the promised Messiah, Christian interpretations of the Hebrew Scriptures rely heavily on Jewish sources. The biblical heroes of Judaism are the heroes of Christendom; Christians as well as Jews see the enemies of the Chosen People as the enemies of God. And the historical background, as well as the significance of specific Scriptures expounded by Jewish scholars, is accepted by their Christian counterparts.

But when it comes to the matter of hunting, there is a wide divergence between Jewish and Christian tradition. The traditional Jewish abhorrence of hunting begins with commentaries on the man called Nimrod. He is the first man the Bible describes as a hunter. (Gen. 10:9) The Rabbis castigated him for this activity and linked it to the general degeneracy of his character. The *Jerusalem Targum* says Nimrod "was mighty in hunting and in sin before God." The *Syriac* calls him "a warlike giant" and the *Targum* of Jonathan ben Uzziel says: "From the foundation of the world none was ever found like Nimrod; powerful in hunting and in rebellions against the Lord."[1]

Along with hunting, Nimrod's "rebellions against the Lord" included his founding of the city of Babel, in which the infamous tower was built. Men believed they had become so technologically proficient that they could construct a building that would "reach unto heaven"—a tower that would give them access to the abode of Deity. The egotism of that undertaking mirrors the arrogance that led men to kill God's creatures as a diversion or as a demonstration of their prowess.

But it is not only the hunter-as-sportsman who is the target of rabbinic contempt. Commentators who castigate Nimrod have little use for that other biblical hunter, Esau, who ate the animals that he killed. Esau was the twin who sold his birthright to his brother Jacob for a bowl of lentils. The Bible describes him as a man who spent his time roaming the land, looking for animals to kill. (Gen. 25:27) But his brother Jacob, who became the Patriarch of the twelve tribes of Israel, is described as living the life of a farmer, tending the crops that fed his extended family.

Esau, like Nimrod, is considered a contemptible character. The *Encyclopedia Judaica* reports that, "The two famous hunters in the Bible, Nimrod and Esau, were regarded in a derogatory light, as 'rebels against God' and the very antithesis of the spirit of Judaism." The *Encyclopedia* also reports that "the rabbinical attitude toward hunting is entirely negative. Harsh things are said about those who hunt even for a living."[2]

This condemnation of hunting and hunters continued to mark Judaism. It gained strength throughout medieval times and by A.D. 1700, *Shemesh Zedakah* (no. 57) forbade hunting with weapons both as a profession and for sport. With regard to the latter, the author, S. Morpurgo, emphatically states that those who hunt "have taken hold of the occupation of Esau the wicked, and are guilty of cruelty in putting to death God's creatures for no reason."[3]

But this ongoing, pervasive condemnation of hunting within Jewish tradition had no parallel among Christians. In fact, Christianity increasingly supported the cruelty that vented itself in hunting. In medieval times it was the wealthy nobles who had the time and the means to indulge their bloodlust by killing animals as a recreational pursuit. And because the churches and their clerics coveted the economic and military support of this privileged class, they blessed this gratuitous slaughter of the innocent. They also officiated at pre-hunt services in the private chapels of the wealthy, asking God for the grace to kill large numbers of His creatures.

The Christian voices that were raised in protest against the wanton murder of animal beings were ignored—even the repugnance toward hunting and hunters that was encoded in Catholic Canon Law was ignored: "Esau was a hunter because he was a sinner; and in the Holy Scriptures we do not find a single holy man being a hunter." (From the *Corpus Juris Canonici*. Rome, 1582.)

In the same century, Saint Thomas More wrote in *Utopia* about the kind of community in which economic, political and social rules "would reflect mankind's decision to live within the framework of God's plan for the earth." The people of this Godly community would learn that they were not "masters, but stewards" of God's creation, and hunting would be forbidden. The inhabitants of this community "would not believe that the divine clemency delights in bloodshed and slaughter, seeing that it has imparted life to animate creatures that they might enjoy life."

But in spite of the many religious spokesmen who have condemned the abuse and murder of animals through the centuries, recreational killing remains an acceptable and honored activity for Christians. Many contemporary churches sponsor hunting programs. Pigeon shoots, raccoon hunts, and other murderous events are planned by these churches as part of their family values programs. Hunting is acclaimed as a unique opportunity for inter-generational bonding, enabling parent and child to spend a day in the woods, enjoying the beauty of God's creation while looking for small creatures to kill.

These outings always begin with prayers that ask God's blessing on the day's activities and are usually followed by the testimonies of those who tell of the gratitude and closeness they feel to the Lord, for having been given the opportunity to enjoy the beauty of His creation. And neither pastor nor congregants protest a spirituality that claims it is enriched by an attempt to kill God's creatures.

Both the "sportsmen" who kill animals in the name of their Creator, and the church officials who encourage this perversion of godliness, are described in the Scriptures:

> They did not believe the truth, but took pleasure in wickedness. . . . They changed the truth of God into a lie. (2 Thess. 2:12, Rom. 1:25)

---

1. Cited in *Clarke's Commentary* by Adam Clarke, LL.D. Published by Abraham Paul for the New York Methodist Book Concern, 1824. p. 86.
2. In "Hunting," p. 1111.
3. Quoted in *Jewish Life in the Middle Ages* by I. Abrahams, Philadelphia: Jewish Publication Society, 1993. pp. 399–400.

Chapter Ten
Thou Shalt not Covet or Steal

THE CONTEMPT FOR GOD'S CREATION THAT IS manifested in the Christian support of recreational killing is further revealed in the wearing of furs. Now that synthetic materials are easily available and are more durable and warmer than animal skins, there is no excuse to slaughter animals for their fur. And in these circumstances, it becomes obvious that people are willing to have animals trapped, clubbed to death, or raised as commodities simply to satisfy their vanity and their greed.

Although greed and avarice are not popular subjects for sermons in a consumer culture, when that greed becomes the impetus for the slaughter of millions of animals it represents a serious, moral evil. The willingness to have animals killed because people lust after the covering given to them by God should be challenged by every religious leader. But it is not.

While churches denounce the violence of television and films, of computer games and Web sites, as detrimental to their children's moral development, the violence perpetrated by adults on helpless animals is ignored. It is gratuitous violence and those young people who have not yet sold their souls to the *status quo* know it for what it is. They, more than their complacent parents, react with horror to the sight of infant seals beaten to death because their snow-white bodies are such a valuable commodity. They are more likely than their parents to remember a news item that shows ranch-raised animals being anally electrocuted in order to preserve the fur for which they have been bred. And they are usually more troubled than their parents by reports of the slow and agonizing deaths of those creatures caught in steel traps.

Yet when it comes to trying to understand why some teenagers refuse to accept the family religion, both parents and pastors ignore any suggestion that this refusal may arise from an unspoken judgment on the part of the young person: A judgment of the immorality of those who easily accept any cruelty that has not been defined as such by their church. Church members would rather believe that the rejection of religion can be traced to a teenage rebellion against restrictive rules and regulations than consider that there are adolescents, as well as adults, who reject a religion because its followers do not maintain a high enough standard of morality.

The same situation existed in the time of Jesus. He called the more conspicuously religious among his people pious hypocrites. Although they scrupulously upheld the rules and regulations of Judaism, they neglected more important matters of justice and mercy (see Matt. 23:23 NIV). Jesus said that the Pharisees spent a great deal of time insuring they did nothing to conflict with the most trivial requirements of their religion, but overlooked more significant issues. Christ put it most succinctly when he told such people: "You strain out a gnat but swallow a camel." (Matt. 23:24 NIV) He also gave a warning to those who relied on religious practices. It was ignored by most of the people of his time, and is still consistently ignored:

> For I say unto you, That except your righteousness shall exceed the righteousness of the scribes and Pharisees, ye shall in no case enter into the kingdom of heaven." (Matt. 5:20)

The righteousness of which Jesus spoke had to do with the treatment of animals as well as of humans. In his time, the abuse of animals was carried out under the guise of sacrificial religion. Jesus did not teach an otherworldly religion; he did not tell his followers to accept the injustices of this world and piously look forward to an afterlife in which goodness and justice would rule. To the contrary, he told his followers that they were to behave in such a way that life on earth would be a reflection of the goodness of the heavenly kingdom. He told them to pray that God's "will be done, on earth as it is in heaven." (Matt. 6:10)

And when he took vigorous action to try and disrupt the sacrificial proceedings at the Jerusalem Temple,[1] he was demonstrating the practicality of that prayer. Clearly, killing terrorized animals in the name of their Creator was not something that would go on in the heavenly realm, so it should not be carried out on earth. Consequently, the cruelty of animal sacrifice was never part of the Christian religion. But two thousand years later, other cruelties are perpetrated on animals by those who piously repeat the Lord's Prayer, asking that life here on earth will reflect the life hereafter.

The cruelties are many, and among the most gratuitous in our culture is the wearing of fur. The same people who are scandalized by reports of youngsters who will kill another child because they covet his sneakers, covet the skins of animals and are willing to have them killed in order to steal their fur. They sit in churches, wearing the evidence of their covetousness and their theft, and no minister or priest challenges this sin of the affluent.

Although the clergy have no direct control over the actions of their congregants, they do have some control over church policy. Drinking and smoking are outlawed within the sanctuaries of churches and there is no reason why the wearing of fur cannot also be forbidden. There is certainly a precedent. Although ministers usually do not speak out against hunting, neither do they generally allow the trophies of recreational killing to be hung in their churches. The heads of deer and other slain creatures are not allowed to adorn the sanctuary walls. Neither should the fur of dead animals adorn the bodies of worshippers.

Instead of treating immorality as if it were primarily a sexual transgression, church leaders need to exercise the kind of leadership that goes beyond such circumscribed definitions. In his own time, Jesus went beyond such judgments: He assailed the religious intolerance that had created a hierarchy of unrighteousness and assigned degrees of sinfulness to a given act.

He was teaching in Jerusalem and the chief priests and elders had challenged his authority. At the end of this ongoing confrontation, Jesus told them: "Verily I say unto you that the publicans and the harlots go into the kingdom of God before you." (Matt. 21:31) To the religiously observant people of his time, tax collectors and prostitutes were numbered among the worst kind of sinners: the publicans for their greed; the harlots for their sexual immorality. And when Jesus said that among such people there were those who were more godly than they, the self-righteously religious became incensed.

In our own time, many who profess to be followers of Christ would be incensed if their pastors told them that worshipping God, clothed in the bodies of His dead creatures, was sinful and immoral. Church leaders will preach against sexual sins even if this brings a negative reaction from the congregation; they hope that such preaching will keep their listeners from the spiritual and physical dangers of promiscuity. However, they do not speak out against nonsexual sins that enjoy a high degree of acceptance among their church members; they are afraid of offending them. But they ought to be concerned about the spiritual dangers of greed and covetousness inherent in the supplying and wearing of furs. They ought to be concerned about the sin of self-righteousness, which is always a temptation for the religiously observant.

Unless these ministers of the Gospel look beyond the narrow circle of traditionally defined sinfulness, they will be like the religious leaders of whom Jesus warned. He said that although these men refused to see the truth themselves, they insisted on trying to lead others in the paths of righteousness and this could only lead to disaster: "[The Pharisees] are blind guides. If a blind man leads a blind man, both will fall into a ditch." (Matt. 15:14)

Unfortunately, the spirit of the Pharisees is alive and well among those ministers who do not challenge the wearing of fur, and among those church members who would never miss a Sunday service but have no qualms about praising God with outstretched arms that are covered with the remains of His dead animals.

---

1. See page 49 onward.

Chapter Eleven
Animal Abuse/Human Abuse

I N THE GARDEN OF EDEN, WHEN THE SERPENT
tempted Eve to eat the forbidden fruit, she initially refused
because "God hath said ye shall not eat of it, neither shall
ye touch it, lest ye die." (Gen. 3:3–4) The serpent countered this
by telling her, "Ye shall not surely die." Of course, Adam and
Eve did eat of the tree, but they did not die. At least not
physically. The Hebrew word used for death is *mooth* and it
signifies either a literal or figurative death. And in what has
become known as the Fall, the couple did die spiritually. They
were estranged from the Lord with whom they had daily
walked in the Garden, and they were estranged from each other.

Still, there was no physical death at this time. And there is
a belief, usually unspoken, that God introduced death into the
world because of human sin. But that is not what the Bible says.
It was man, not God, who brought death into the world. Abel
killed a lamb and Cain killed a man. From the beginning, the

violence directed towards animals and the violence that humans direct towards each other have been inextricably linked.[1]

But in spite of this biblical witness, many people resent any suggestion that the horrors inflicted on human beings by their own species can in any way be compared with the suffering of animal beings. And although there is a refusal to even consider such a comparison, the Bible does not hesitate to make that connection. The prophet Habakkuk, speaking in the name of God, clearly made the association:

> For the violence done to Lebanon is going to overwhelm you, so will the slaughter of its terrified beasts; you have shed men's blood and ravished the city and all [creatures] who live in it. (Hab. 2:17 JB)

This linking of the fate of animals and humans is an ongoing biblical theme. Jeremiah stood at the gate of the Jerusalem Temple and related the killing of helpless animals and the oppression of powerless humans beings:

> If ye oppress not the stranger, the fatherless, and the widow, and shed not innocent blood in this place [by animal sacrifice] I will cause you to dwell in that land that I gave to your fathers, for ever and ever. (Jer. 7:6–7)

A century earlier, the prophet Jonah was told by God of His concern for both the human and animal inhabitants of Nineveh. It was an Assyrian city that had been spared destruction, and the Jewish prophet was not pleased by this divine reprieve. The Lord reproved him for this self-centeredness, saying: "Am I not to feel sorry for Nineveh, the great city, in which there are more than a hundred and twenty thousand people who cannot tell their right hand from their left, to say nothing of all the animals?" (Jon. 4:11)

In the Book of Ecclesiastes, the fate of animals and of humans is linked together in their lives, and in their deaths:

> Man's fate is like that of the animals: the same fate awaits them both: As one dies, so dies the other. All have the same breath [spirit]. . . . Who knows if the spirit of man rises upward and if the spirit of the animal goes down into the earth? (Eccles. 3:19, 21 NIV)

The above-quoted scripture is not a favorite of religious leaders. Although, as with other biblical verses, there has been an effort to twist its meaning, no one has yet been able to explain away "man has no advantage over the animals." (Eccles. 3:19)

Although Man has no preeminence above an animal, that has not stopped human beings from exerting a brutal and relentless dominion over animals. Speaking for God, the prophet Amos indicted his people for the violence being perpetrated on animals in the rituals of sacrificial religion:

> When you offer me *holocausts*, I reject your oblations and refuse to look at your sacrifices of fattened cattle . . . but let justice flow like water and integrity like an unfailing stream." (Amos 5:22 JB emphasis added)

"Holocaust" is the term used to designate the "burnt offerings" of animals as described in the Book of Leviticus. These animals had to be totally immolated, so the fire on the altars where their bodies lay burned day and night. Their ashes were allowed to accumulate, until room had to be made for the next batch of remains.

In our own time, the death of millions of people killed in Nazi prison camps and then burned to ashes is called the Holocaust. At places like Auschwitz and Dachau it is reported that smoke from the ovens was ever-present, that they burned day and night. Applying a term that was first used to describe the death of countless other species underscores the fact that Nazi prisoners were treated like animals. They were herded into boxcars "like cattle," and, like animals who are transported to their deaths, the people also thirsted and had no water. They hungered, and had no food. And they had no room to move; no way to rest. No way to avoid living in the midst of their own waste.

But although the word *holocaust* links the fate of animals with the horrors suffered by humans, there has been no hint of compassion for these other sentient beings, who continue to be treated as disposable "things." With very few exceptions, there has been no attempt to understand the moral/ethical relationship between a claim that animals can be tormented and slaughtered in the best interests of the human race and the Nazi claim that prisoners were brutalized and murdered because that served the best interests of an emerging super race.

One of those who did understand this relationship was Nobel prize winner Isaac Bashevis Singer. He wrote: "As long as human beings go on shedding the blood of animals, there will never be any peace. There is only one little step from killing animals to creating gas chambers à la Hitler and concentration camps à la Stalin. There will be no justice as long as man will stand with a knife or a gun and destroy those who are weaker than he is."[2]

But Singer's profound understanding of the ineradicable link between killing powerless animals and the killing of powerless humans is not recognized by the medical profession nor by social and behavioral scientists. Although they have lately noticed a connection between the abuse of animals by children and their subsequent abuse of other people, there is little concern for the suffering of animals. Like the formulators of Christian doctrine,[3] these formulators of secular doctrine are more concerned with the damage done to human society when people brutalize other creatures than they are by the suffering inflicted on these sentient creatures. They are not concerned about the animals who are tortured: They want to find ways to stop this cruelty from spreading to human victims.

This is not surprising. Many health professionals have been desensitized to the suffering of animals because they have been trained under circumstances in which they witnessed, and acquiesced to, sadistic experiments on them. They have been participants in a system of ritualistic abuse in which the same atrocities are endlessly repeated, with the same predictable results. Nothing new is learned; no breakthrough is made. The emotional and physical torment of all kinds of creatures—dogs, cats, monkeys, rabbits, and mice—is carried out in the name of education and research. And at the same time that human chauvinism claims a unique place among the species of the earth—a superior development—these "lesser" creatures are endlessly tortured and killed with the claim that it is done to facilitate an understanding of human physiology and psychology.

In an effort to give a religious significance to the work they do, vivisectors never use the word "kill" when referring to the slaughter of laboratory animals: They call it "sacrificing" them. This is the term used by doctors and other vivisectors and is *de rigueur* when referring to the killing of those creatures whose torment is finally ended by their death. Clad in their white garments, like the priests of old, they have become the leaders of our modern sacrificial cult.

In our contemporary Western culture, people do not worry overmuch about their souls. Most are quite confident that they are in good shape spiritually and that God is well pleased with them.[4] Consequently, they are unlikely to believe their religious leaders have to sacrifice animals in the temple of their God, in order to expiate for their sins. However, they are very much concerned about their bodies. So our secular, sacrificial cult is well funded and flourishing in the hallowed halls of research and in medical institutes all over the world.

In biblical times there was no way to prove a correlation between animal sacrifice, the staying of God's wrath, or the buying of His favor. It was enough that the claim was made. It did not have to be proven. The same is true of scientism. Almost daily, an important "possible breakthrough" that supposedly comes as a result of animal sacrifice is announced. The breakthrough is always "possible" and the announcer is always careful to say it "might" be useful in treating human disease—"several years from now." And although the same claim has been made for decades, and the human benefits do not materialize, it does not matter. Like its religious predecessor, the secular cult of sacrifice is firmly established on a belief system that was developed to preserve it.

In spite of prophetic pronouncements to the contrary, the ancients chose to believe the priests who said that the deaths of countless animals, on the altars of God, would save them from the penalties of sin. And in spite of promised, miraculous cures that fail to come about, their modern counterparts believe that the mutilation and death of countless animals, on the altars of scientism, will save them from the ravages of accident, disease, or old age.

But there is a biblical pronouncement that warns: "Be not deceived, God is not mocked; whatsoever a man soweth, that shall he also reap." (Gal. 6:7) It is the religious formulation of a timeless moral law, at work in the universe. It is a law that is often ignored, and even when its terms are eventually carried out there is a refusal to recognize the causal connection between what has been sown and what is being reaped.

In biblical times the people refused to heed either the prophets who spoke out against animal sacrifice, or the Christ who tried to dismantle that system. And when historical forces brought about the destruction of the Jerusalem Temple it was not only the priests and others who profited from the cult who suffered. Those who had acquiesced in the ongoing slaughter of animals, in the name of God, also suffered. "Like animals" they were driven from the land that had been their home. Like animals, they suffered the fear and dread of any living creature who knows it is being hunted down by those who will show it no mercy. Like animals, people were tortured and slaughtered by men who had neither remorse nor compunction for what they were doing.

In our own time, many voices—including those of medical and mental health professionals—have been raised in condemnation of the atrocities that vivisectors commit.[5] Books and other materials detail the medical and economic fraud of those who garner billions of tax dollars to finance their work. But these modern prophets[6] are faced with the hostility of a populace that has been carefully taught to believe that the salvation of their bodies is dependent upon the continuation of the medical, sacrificial cult.

Even as evidence mounts that a worldwide plague like AIDS can be traced to animal experimentation,[7] all the powers of press and propaganda align themselves in the fight to suppress or distort these truths. But like the Temple sacrifices of old, the modern travesty of vivisection will end in accord with universal law: What we sow we shall reap.

But there is another moral law at work in the universe—the law of love and compassion. When human beings stop abusing other creatures, the animals will no longer retaliate: "In that day I will make a covenant for them with the beasts of the field and the birds of the air and the creatures that move along the ground." This interspecies nonviolence will be reflected in a peaceful accord between human beings: "Bow and sword and battle I will abolish from the land so that all may lie down in safety." (Hos. 2:18 NIV) But the fulfillment of this prophecy depends upon human choices.

Throughout the Bible, there is the explicit teaching that women and men are capable of choosing between good and evil. They can manifest the violence and aggression that brings destruction in its wake, or they can manifest the goodness and compassion that can bring about the peaceable kingdom. But this has never been a popular teaching and, in contemporary times, the refusal to accept its premise has been given a pseudo-scientific basis. The claim is made that poor, struggling human beings are beset by a barbaric past in which violence was a way of life. So, of course, our society is chaotic; humankind has not yet outgrown its aggressive behavior. But this rationalization ignores the fact that a barbaric past was the result of the human choice to manifest aggression rather than compassion.

This secular rationalization is mirrored by a religious refusal to accept responsibility for a violent world, and a pseudo-biblical excuse has been devised to support this refusal. It claims that human beings are doomed to make war, slaughter, pillage, and rape "until Jesus comes." But in the meantime, those who live by this scenario feel no need to make the choices, or the laws, that would help to bring about a world in which aggression and violence are unacceptable expressions of human behavior—under whatever guise or excuse they are indulged.

For thousands of years, prophetic voices have called upon men and women to renounce their aggression and the oppression of the powerless, whether human or animal:

> The multitude of your sacrifices—what are they to me? says the Lord. . . . Your hands are full of blood; wash and make yourselves clean. Take your evil deeds out of my sight! *Stop doing wrong*, learn to do right! Seek justice, *rebuke the oppressor*. Defend the cause of the fatherless, plead the case of the widow. (Isa. 1:11, 15–17 NIV emphasis added)

The oracles of Isaiah and other prophets are a call to justice and compassion but, when that call is ignored, their words become an indictment of those who refuse to "stop doing wrong." It also becomes an indictment of an entire society that not only refuses to "rebuke the oppressor" in its midst, but actively supports those who maim, torture, and kill the least powerful among us, in the irrational and immoral belief that inflicting disease, deprivation, and death on other creatures will bring health, abundance, and longevity to human beings.

The evidence that shows far too many physiological, cellular, genetic and psychological variations between species for accurate and predictive extrapolation to humans is ignored. The hundreds of millions of dollars awarded to individuals and institutions brings with it the kind of power and prestige that compromises objectivity and insures that effective studies which do not use animal-to-human research are ignored or underfunded. So the human suffering that could be alleviated if effective research methods were used continues.

This refusal to acknowledge the relationship between the ongoing suffering of humans and the gratuitous torment of research animals insures that the ancient warning about retribution continues to be a self-fulfilling prophecy in our own day: "The merciful, kind and generous man benefits himself, for his deeds return to bless him, but he who is cruel and callous to others brings retribution on himself." (Proverbs 11:17 AMP)

------

1. Even if a corrupt text and the misleading translations of Genesis 4:1–8, which tell this story are accepted, the fact remains that animal and human murder stand juxtaposed at the beginning of human history.
2. Quoted in the preface to *Vegetarianism: A Way of Life* by Dudley Giehl, 1979.
3. "Man has no duties toward animals because they have no independent personalities. . . . It is sinful, however, to cause an animal needless suffering. The sinfulness does not lie in a violation of the animal's rights but in a person's irrational conduct, since reason forbids causing unnecessary pain and death. Moreover, cruelty to animals has a brutalizing effect on the tormentor." *Modern Catholic Dictionary* edited by John A. Hardon, S.J. Garden City, NY: Doubleday & Co. 1980.
4. In the United States, polls indicate that more than 95 percent of those who believe in an afterlife that includes a hell are quite confident that they will not go there.
5. See Bibliography for a partial list.
6. Often called whistle-blowers.
7. *The River: A Journey to the Source of HIV and AIDS* by Edward Hooper. Little, Brown and Company, 1999.

Appendix
The Origin of Sacrifice

TRADITIONAL EXPLANATIONS OF SACRIFICIAL religion attribute its practice to the naiveté of "primitive" people who believed that such sacrifices were pleasing to God. But that explanation has nothing to do with the origin of sacrifice. It only restates what the Bible says about the matter. And by the time that the Pentateuch—the first five books of the Bible—was compiled, the consumption of animal flesh had been legitimized for millennia by associating carnivorism with the worship of God.

Eventually, sacrificial religion served other hidden agendas[1] but initially it was the subterfuge humans used to indulge their lust for flesh.[2] In the same way that the prohibition against killing other human beings was overcome by murdering them in the name of Holy Wars, so also the divine stipulation that mankind only consume the fruits of the earth for its sustenance was overcome by "sacrificing" the animals to God before eating their flesh.

The system of distribution of the dead animals exposes sacrificial religion as an obvious pretext for satisfying an unlawful lust for flesh: God got the suet and intestines while the people kept the most desirable body parts for themselves.

The regulations concerning this division of flesh were quite explicit:

> Then this is what [the priest] is to offer as a burnt offering for Yahweh: the fat that covers the entrails, all the fat that is on the entrails, the two kidneys, the fat that is on them and on the loins, the fatty mass which he will remove from the liver and kidneys. The priest must burn these pieces on the altar as food, as a burnt offering for Yahweh. All the fat belongs to Yahweh. (Lev. 3:14–17 JB)

Although cereal and vegetable offerings were also made to Yahweh, animal sacrifice was the focus and purpose of Israel's elaborate rituals.[3] Ultimately, the sacrificial cult was a system of raising and slaughtering animals for consumption. Regulations forbidding the import into Jerusalem of any livestock that could not be sacrificed and eaten were strictly enforced. Prohibited was the import "of mules, or of horses or of asses . . . or leopards or fox or hares, and in general, that of any animal which is forbidden for the Jews to eat . . . nor let any such animal be bred up in the city. Let them only be permitted to use the sacrifices derived from their fathers, with which they have been obliged to make acceptable atonements to God."[4]

Trade in livestock was such a major factor in Jewish life that all cattle within a five-mile radius of the city were regarded as destined for sacrifice. And because the right to the choicest body parts of the slaughtered animals was a perquisite of being a priest, the kind of illnesses induced by a meat-heavy diet were endemic to the priesthood.[5]

Of course, the endless slaughter of animals is accompanied by copious amounts of blood: the clothing, the person, and the earth itself bore witness to the butchery that was taking place. And since there was no way to avoid this witness, human beings decreed that the shedding of blood was sacred and most pleasing to God. So the Temple at Jerusalem—perceived to be the special abode of Deity—became, in effect, a giant slaughterhouse, awash in the blood of its victims.

The Mishnah marvels at how many people and animals could be packed into the Temple precincts, saying that it was the eighth of the ten wonders of the Holy Place that there was enough room for them all.[6]

In such close confines, there was no escaping the horror of the massacre that took place. If human beings had not convinced themselves that God demanded this slaughter they could not have participated in it. Aiding them in this self-deception was the investiture of the priesthood with all the accouterments of the sacred. For the most part, it was the priests who killed the animals and, because they did this in the exercise of their priestly office, they were perceived to be functioning as servants of the Lord, rather than as butchers.

Although religious leaders insisted that the slaughter of animals was a cornerstone of the relationship to Yahweh, Judaism has survived for almost two thousand years without the rituals of sacrificial religion. But without the status of the priesthood and the imprimatur of God to give it an exalted status, the butchering of animals is no longer seen as a sacred calling. Consequently, human beings have found other ways to distance themselves from its brutality.

We have increasingly hidden the slaughterhouse, and its victims, from sight. Very few persons have any direct experience of the violence and brutality that is inflicted on animals in order to satisfy a carnivorous population. Additionally, the steaks, chops, hamburgers, and cold cuts that are consumed show little resemblance to the creature who had to be killed in order to obtain them. Rarely does the whole carcass of an animal appear on the plate. But even when it does, there is still a religious mechanism in place to help overcome any feelings of guilt. A blessing is pronounced over the meal: God is thanked for providing the dead animal.

To thank God for the fruits of the earth, given to human beings for their sustenance is a legitimate religious act. But to thank the Lord for providing the flesh of an animal is not legitimate. The eating of flesh is a perversion of God's law, indulged by a fallen human race. And to thank God for providing such food is the modern equivalent of sacrificial religion; it represents a continuing determination to claim God's blessing on the slaughter, and consumption, of His creatures.

---

1. The continuation of an hereditary priesthood/leadership and the provision of an outlet for violence and brutality, among other things.
2. As early as A.D. 195 the Christian theologian Clement of Alexandria wrote that "Sacrifices were invented by men to be a pretext for eating flesh."
3. See *The International Standard Bible Encyclopedia* (Grand Rapids: Eerdmans, 1979), v. 4, p. 266.
4. Flavius Josephus. *Antiquities* (Grand Rapids: Kregel Publications, 1978), 12.146.
5. Joachim Jeremias. *Jerusalem in the Time of Jesus* (Philadelphia: Fortress Press, 1969), pp. 26, 106, 170.
6. Mishnah (tractate Aboth), v. 5.

Bibliography

Albright, W. F. *The Biblical Period from Abraham to Ezra*. New York: Harper & Row, 1963.

Baron, Sale W. *A Social and Religious History of the Jews*. New York: Columbia University Press, 1958.

Barton, George. *The Religion of Israel*. New York: Macmillan, 1918.

Bernstein, Leon. *Flavius Josephus: His Time and His Critics*. New York: Liveright Corporation, 1938.

Bright, John. *A History of Israel*, Third edition. Philadelphia: Westminster Press, 1972.

Bruce, F. F. *Israel and the Nations*. Grand Rapids: Eerdmans, 1969.

Buber, Martin. *The Prophetic Faith*. New York: Harper & Row, 1960.

Davidson, A. B. *The Theology of the Old Testament*. Edinburgh: T. & T. Clark, 1949.

de Vaux, Roland. *The Early History of Israel: To the Period of the Judges*. Philadelphia: Westminster Press, 1976.

Finkelstein, Louis. *The Pharisees: The Sociological Background of Their Faith.* Two volumes. Philadelphia: The Jewish Publication Society of America, 1946.

Foerster, Werner. *From the Exile to the Christ: A Historical Introduction to Palestinian Judaism.* Philadelphia: Fortress Press, 1964.

Graetz, H. *History of the Jews.* Philadelphia: The Jewish Publishing Society of America, 1893.

Heschel, Abraham J. *The Prophets.* New York: Harper & Row, 1963.

Jeremias, Joachim. *Jerusalem in the Time of Jesus.* Philadelphia: Fortress Press, 1969.

Kadushin, Maz. *The Rabbinic Mind.* New York: The Jewish Theological Seminary of America, 1952.

Kaufmann, Yehezkel. *The Religion of Israel: From Its Beginnings to the Babylonian Exile.* Chicago: University of Chicago Press, 1960.

Kohler, Kaufmann. *Jewish Theology.* New York: Macmillan, 1932.

Manson, T. W. *The Teaching of Jesus: Studies in Form and Content.* Cambridge: Cambridge University Press, 1955.

Noth, Martin. *The History of Israel.* New York: Harper & Brothers, 1960.

Reicke, Bo. *The New Testament Era: The World of the Bible from 500 BC to AD 100.* Philadelphia: Fortress Press, 1968.

Weber, Max. *Ancient Judaism.* New York: The Free Press, 1952.

Wright, Ernest F. *The Challenge of Israel's Faith.* Chicago: Chicago University Press, 1944.

Recommended Reading

Akers, Keith. *A Vegetarian Sourcebook*. Denver CO: Vegetarian Press, 1993.

Evans, Rose, and Valeria Evans. *Friends of All Creatures*. San Francisco: Sea Fog Press, 1984.

Kalechovsky, Roberta. *Vegetarian Judaism: A Guide for Everyone*. Marblehead, MA: Micah Publications, 1998.

————. ed. *Judaism and Animal Rights: Classical and Contemporary Responses*. Marblehead, MA: Micah Publications, 1992.

Kowalski, Gary. *The Souls of Animals*. Walpole, NH: Stillpoint Publications, 1999.

Linzey, Andrew. *Animal Gospel*. Louisville: Westminster John Knox, 1999.

————. *Animal Theology*. Urbana, IL: Illinois University Press, 1995.

Linzey, Andrew, and Dorothy Yamamoto, eds. *Animals on the Agenda*. Urbana, IL: Illinois University Press, 1998.

McDaniel, Jay. *Of God and Pelicans: A Theology of Reverence for Life*. Louisville: Westminster John Knox, 1989.

Murti, Vasu. *They Shall Not Hurt or Destroy: Animal Rights and Vegetarianism in the Western Religious Traditions*. Available from 30 Villanova Lane, Oakland, CA 94611, 1995. Also www.jesusveg.org

Pinches, Charles, and Jay McDaniel, eds. *Good News for Animals?: Christian Approaches to Animal Well-Being*. Maryknoll, NY: Orbis, 1993.

Regan, Tom, ed. *Animal Sacrifices: Religious Perspectives on the Use of Animals in Science*. Philadelphia: Temple University Press, 1988.

Rosen, Steven, ed. *Diet for Transcendence: Vegetarianism and the World Religions*. Badger, CA: Torchlight, 1996.

Rowe, Martin, ed. *The Way of Compassion: Vegetarianism, Environmentalism, Animal Advocacy, and Social Justice*. New York: Stealth Technologies, 1999.

Ruesch, Hans. *Naked Empress or the Great Medical Fraud*. Switzerland: Civis Publications, 1982.

————. *Slaughter of the Innocent: Animals in Medical Research, the Myth, the Perpetrators, the Damage to Human Health*. New York: Bantam, 1978. (Both Ruesch titles are distributed in U.S. by The Nature of Wellness, P.O. Box 10400, Glendale, CA 91209-3400.)

Schwartz, Richard. *Judaism and Vegetarianism*. New York: Lantern Books, 2000.

Skriver, Carl Anders. *The Forgotten Beginnings of Creation and Christianity*. Denver: Vegetarian Press, 1990.

Spencer, Colin. *The Heretic's Feast: A History of Vegetarianism*. Hanover, NH: University Press of New England, 1995.

Recommended Reading

Vaclavik, Charles P. *The Vegetarianism of Jesus Christ: The Pacifism, Communalism and Vegetarianism of Primitive Christianity.* Three Rivers, CA: Kaweah Publications, 1989.

Webb, Stephen H. *On God and Dogs: A Christian Theology of Compassion for Animals.* New York: Oxford University Press, 1997.

Westbeau, Georges H. *Little Tyke: The True Story of a Gentle Vegetarian Lionness.* New York: Theosophical Publishing House, 1986.

Young, Richard Alan. *Is God a Vegetarian? Christianity, Vegetarianism, and Animal Rights.* Chicago: Open Court Publishing, 1999.

Of related interest from Lantern Books

Keith Akers

The Lost Religion of Jesus
Simple Living and Nonviolence in Early Christianity

Akers argues that Jewish Christianity was vegetarian and practiced pacifism and communal living.

"A whole new conception of Christianity."—**Walter Wink**

Marc Bekoff

Strolling with Our Kin
Speaking for and Respecting Voiceless Animals
Foreword by Jane Goodall

"A philosophical and ethical odyssey that examines how we can all live in harmony with our kindred creatures."—*The Animals' Agenda*

Gary Kowalski

The Bible According to Noah
Theology as If Animals Mattered

Kowalski explores the ancient stories of the Bible to examine their relevance today—especially in regard to how we view and treat other animals.

Richard H. Schwartz, Ph.D.

Judaism and Global Survival

"A shofar calling the Jewish community to wake up to current crises and at the same time return to our roots."—**Mark X. Jacobs**

Richard H. Schwartz, Ph.D.
Judaism and Vegetarianism
New Revised Edition

"Schwartz has made a case that is difficult to refute, in a book you will find difficult to ignore."—*Jerusalem Post*
"Fully documented and very convincing . . . A well-done treatise on a subject of increasing interest."—*Library Journal*

Steven Rosen
Holy Cow
The Hare Krishna Contribution to Vegetarianism and Animal Rights

Hinduism scholar Steven Rosen explores the world of the Hare Krishna movement, which has been instrumental in raising awareness of vegetarianism and the plight of animals in the United States.

Norm Phelps
The Great Compassion
Buddhism and Animal Rights

The Great Compassion studies the different strains of Buddhism and the sutras that command respect for all life. Norm Phelps, a longtime student of Buddhism and acquaintance of His Holiness the Dalai Lama, answers the central questions of whether Buddhism demands vegetarianism or whether the Buddha ate meat

At your bookstore or from the publisher:
Lantern Books
1 Union Square West, Suite 201
New York, NY 10003
212-414-2275
www.lanternbooks.com